Translating Tradition

Other readers featured in the "Longman Topics" series include:

Translating Tradition

KAREN E. BEARDSLEE
Burlington County College of New Jersey

New York   San Francisco   Boston
London   Toronto   Sydney   Tokyo   Singapore   Madrid
Mexico City   Munich   Paris   Cape Town   Hong Kong   Montreal

Senior Vice President and Publisher: Joseph Opiela
Acquisitions Editor: Susan Kunchandy
Marketing Manager: Deborah Murphy
Managing Editor: Bob Ginsberg
Project Coordination, Text Design, and Electronic Page Makeup:
    Sunflower Publishing Services
Cover Design Manager: Nancy Danahy
Cover Photo: "Hand-Tinted Family Photos on Desk," photograph by
    Patricia Ridenour, © The Image Bank/Getty Images, Inc.
Manufacturing Buyer: Lucy Hebard
Printer and Binder: RR Donnelley & Sons Company
Cover Printer: Phoenix Color Corporation

For permission to use copyrighted material, grateful acknowledg-
ment is made to the copyright holders on pp. 199–202, which are
hereby made part of this copyright page.

Library of Congress Cataloging-in-Publication Data
    Translating tradition / [edited by] Karen E. Beardslee.
        p. cm.
    Includes bibliogaphical references.
    ISBN 0-321-10577-X
        1. Folklore—Authorship. 2. Communication in folklore.
    3. Storytelling. 4. Family. 5. Community life. I. Beardslee,
    Karen E., 1965–

    GR44.5.T73 2004
    808′.0663982—dc21   2003047732

Please visit our website at http://www.ablongman.com

ISBN 0-321-10577-X

12345678910-DOH-06050403

Contents

CHAPTER 5
Traditional Processes 93

CHAPTER 6
Traditions: A Changing Same 117

Description

Narration

Our world is rich in lore—those traditions we engage in because they give our lives structure and meaning. More than matters of habit, our rituals, stories, annual gatherings, crafts, and foodways, for instance, help us define ourselves as individuals and as family and community members. Although we may not be aware of it, folklore is one of the most important ways we connect to the past, negotiate the present, and envision the future. Folklorists continually seek to convey folklore's role in shaping our lives. The readings that make up this book contribute to that effort, as will the explorations, discussions, and writings you will be encouraged to do in response to those readings. In other words, the purpose of *Translating Tradition* is to promote the value of folklore.

Our families and communities are as diverse as are the people who make them up. And, because virtually every one of us is invested in a family and/or community structure of some sort, we have at our disposal an abundant source of traditions to explore and discuss in writing. Each family, each community to which an individual attaches him or herself engages in traditions that are both particular to that family or community and similar to the traditions of other families and communities. What's more, the lore of all groups gains substance through the understandings, explanations, and expectations attached to it. When we participate in studies of family and community folklore, we become interactive scholars, enthusiastic to discover those traditions we have in common—*"You mean to tell me your neighborhood has an in-the-park crack-of-dawn Easter Egg hunt, too? I thought my community was the only one to do such a crazy thing!"* We also become in-depth researchers—*"I'll have to ask my grandmother about her Krustals recipe. I know it has been handed down for genera-*

tions." Moreover, in essence, as we reflect on folklore, as we learn to critically analyze its purpose and value, we become our own cultural scribes—*"My family originated in Tuscany. From there, my great grandparents brought to America the tradition of growing our own vegetables, fruits, and herbs. Each year I help my father prepare for planting. This is one of my favorite things to do because it gives me a chance to spend time with my dad. The work itself, although it is hard and continues throughout the growing and harvesting seasons, reminds me of my ancestors in Italy and makes me feel a part of something larger, a cultural community that goes beyond my own backyard."* I think you will truly enjoy, as my former students have, talking about the folklore in your own life. I hope you will be an attentive listener when others do so as well. In this reader you will encounter authors, essayists, and poets who focus on the relevance of folk culture. After reading their works, I believe that not only will you want to discuss all of this folklore "stuff" (as one student puts it), all of your folklore findings, you will be eager to write about these things as well. And as I tell my own students, wanting to write can make all the difference when it comes to writing well.

THE FOLKLORE FOCUS IN THE COLLEGE CLASSROOM: THE INVESTED SELF

While writing about folklore may not necessarily make writing itself easier, writing about those family and/or community traditions in which you are involved and invested can lead to a more positive experience with the writing process. Two years ago, during my first folklore-focused composition course, students were asked to write a letter to me (they did not have to reveal their identity in the letter if they did not want to) evaluating the use of folklore studies in the composition classroom. I was pleased to find that an overwhelming majority of the students felt the focus on folklore had made their encounter with the writing process more enjoyable. Note, for instance, what former student Blake Hacking had to say about his folklore-focused writing experience:

Dear Dr. Beardslee:

I do believe that a good way to get a student's creative juices flowing is to incorporate folklore into his/her writing. It keeps them interested in what they're writing about and that, in turn, produces well-written essays. I have a few examples of how it has helped me and why I think you should continue combining folklore studies with the writing courses you teach.

There are many different types of folklore, but the kind of folklore this class got me interested in is Family Folklore. I have found that folklore is all around me at home. When my father tells me jokes his father told him, when my mother tells me about her life as a child, when I tell my parents how much fun I had in Dr. B's English class all semester, I am taking part in the art of folklore. I have learned that the stories told by my grandparents, that putting up Christmas decorations each year, and that even some of the meals I eat are all examples of Family Folklore.

Folklore is useful in a writing class because it keeps the students involved in what they are writing about. When students aren't interested in what they are writing about, they won't pay attention to the writing itself, thus causing a poor grade. For instance, if students can write about what they do during the holidays with their families, I can pretty much guarantee most students will be interested in the topic and have a more enjoyable writing experience. This, in turn, may help students produce a better grade.

All throughout high school, I had to write on topics I did not care for at all. This semester in college, however, it has been a different story. I was able to write about the subject that I have the most experience with, my family.

Writing through folklore, I feel, has improved my writing skills. Now that I am interested, I care about what I'm writing and want it to be the best it can be. I don't want to write a half-effort paper because I now know that my writing represents me and what I care about most. These days I proofread my papers thoroughly and work to revise them so I am sure I am saying what I mean and making what I see in my head clear to my reader. I do all this now not only to pick up little mistakes, but also because as I read it is fun to relive in my mind again the traditions I've written about and the memories I have of those things.

I've learned a lot about my family through folklore and how important our traditions are and why we practice them. But not only did I learn about my family through this class and its focus on folklore, I've learned about myself as well. The bond that I share with my grandfather is stronger and I realize what an important role I play in our family traditions. Folklore helps me learn more about my family and myself and it makes me aware of how lucky I am to have the family I do. Thank you, Dr. B.

Your student, Blake Hacking

As Blake indicates in his letter, chronicling folk traditions is a way of visiting them—of bringing them to life in the here and now on paper. And as you strive to do your traditions justice, to awaken the past in the present, to tell the story as it was told, to re-create the garden in all its backbreaking and lush glory, you are, truth be told, not only trying to get things right as you write, but you are honing your writing skills—trying to get the writing right. Right?

Translating Tradition encourages the previously described constructive student–writing relationship, as well as the aforementioned explorations of self, community, and culture. The readings of the book are grouped according to common themes, but you are introduced to each chapter with a brief discussion of that chapter's folklore focus, collaborative work in group activities, and cross-cultural sharing in class discussion. Each reading is introduced by a brief biographical head note that places the author in a particular social and cultural context. After each selection there are three analysis/writing assignments ("My Thoughts in Writing") to promote critical analysis and thoughtful discussion, to encourage comparisons of folklore forms, and to highlight specific rhetorical elements of the text. In addition, at the end of each chapter, you will find three to six synthesis assignments ("The Readings Come Together") that ask you to compare the selections and a set of suggestions ("There's Something More out There") for further reading.

Each thematic chapter contains readings from a variety of genres, including fiction, poetry, essay, and personal memoir. Several features of the book will help you apply the readings to your study of family and community folklore, your development of critical analysis skills, and your practice of writing. The "My Thoughts in Writing" sections provide you with an opportunity to create more structured responses to what you have read and to express what you have learned through guided writing and discussion activities. "The Readings Come Together" sections give you an opportunity to compare and contrast the chapter's selections, and the "There's Something More out There" sections encourage you to do more folklore reading and research and to continue practicing your writing technique. There, you will find assignments requiring you to conduct interviews, to engage in discussion and debate, to define your position, to come to your own conclusions.

Your family and community folklore has much to offer you—as an individual, as a family and community member, as a budding scholar. *Translating Tradition* asks you to look inward and open outward, to become a reader and a writer of works that speak to, record, and affirm the value of folklore in everyday life.

KAREN E. BEARDSLEE

Translating Tradition

Recognizing Folklore

When you hear the word *folklore*, do you think about stories and storytelling? If so, you are on the right track because the stories we tell and pass on from one generation to the next are a part of folklore—but they are only one part of a much larger whole. You see, folklore is also the gardening your neighbor does or the quilting for which your aunt is known. You see, Folklore is also the gardening your neighbor does or the guilting for which your aunt is known. It is the annual Christmas-tree-picking outing your family goes on each December or the community Canoe Race held each July at the lake. It is the weekly Sunday dinner at your grandparent's house and the scrapbooks you fill with carefully chosen mementos—items from special family or community occasions that initiate the stories you would eventually like to share with others, perhaps even your own children. It is the modern dance your co-worker loves so much and the jazz your mother is teaching your brother to play on his guitar. In general, we say that folklore encompasses so much of what we do to organize our days and infuse our lives with meaning. But we must remember the specificity of folklore—the fact that folklore comprises those habits of thought or behavior that come to us via word of mouth and/or customary example. Although there are always exceptions, most folklore forms are considered "traditional, unofficial, noninstitutional" parts of culture (Brunvand 1986, 4–9). That is, they are not learned in classroom settings or from instructional manuals. They are conveyed through oral communication, person-to-person interaction, hands-on creation, hearts-in experience.

THE FOLKLORE OF YOUR FOLK

The types of folklore you will be studying and writing about are family and community folklore, with the understanding that family and community may be defined differently by different people. These two areas of folklore are the primary focus because traditions and customs shape so many of our family and community experiences. Family and community folklore are different from family and community history, for, while our histories are presented as unchanging chronicles of past events, our folklore (be it a story, a photograph, a tradition, or a custom, for example) is by nature both fixed *and* changing. We transform our experiences into stories, traditions, customs, and behaviors—codify them in forms, which can be easily recalled, retold, and enjoyed for generations to come. But there is a kind of unspoken understanding among family and community members that allows for the reshaping of these forms over time according to the family's or the community's needs and desires (Zeitlin, Kotkin, Baker 1982, 2–3). Take, for instance, my family's yearly Christmas Eve celebration. The general layout of this tradition has remained the same since it first began over fifteen years ago. Yet, like me, the members of my family fully understand, readily accept, and sometimes eagerly anticipate the way this tradition changes a bit from year to year, given the shifts in circumstances as the years progress. Every Christmas Eve, the members of my father's side of the family gather in my grandmother's living room for our annual gift exchange. No matter from where particular family members may be traveling, all of us are sure to be present in my grandmother's kitchen at 6:30 P.M. on December 24th. In that cozy room, individual voices become a part of the general cacophony. On this night, everyone speaks at once as we load our plates with the same stuff served year after year on this occasion: heaping bowls of steamed spiced shrimp; plates of cold cuts, cheeses, and deli rolls; my Aunt Lois's weenie wraps; my grandmother's crunchy cream-cheese potatoes and fudge assortment dish; my home-made candy and cookie tray, as well as my special pepperoni bread; my sister's potato chips and onion dip; and my step-mother's fruit salad. After we have stuffed ourselves to burst-ing, a feat that takes but an hour, we congregate in the living room for the opening of gifts. Used to be, when I was a young girl, gifts would be distributed and each person would open one gift at a time so that the giver could witness the joy his or her gift engendered. But as the family aged, this aspect of the tradition changed. Now we get our individual piles of gifts and simply dig in; everyone opens their pile at once, and there is barely a moment of silence as thank you's are yelled across the room or whispered from person to person, depending on where members are situated in relation to each other. Often I don't even know when my gifts to my family members have been opened and whether the recipients liked what I got them. Nevertheless, on this night, my sense of family is reaffirmed. While the changes wrought by time, distance, births, deaths, and tastes will continue to transform this tradition as the years go by, the tradition maintains a kind of "same old, same old" feel that is a source of immeasurable comfort to us all.

At this moment, perhaps you are feeling as some of my students have felt when first asked to investigate and write about their family and/or community folklore. On more than one occasion, when I have given students their first folklore-focused writing assignment, a few have taken me aside to pro-claim: "But, Dr. Beardslee, my family doesn't have any traditions!" My student Lisa Desjardins made just such a proclamation. I suggested that she interview her mother and her father about the things they do or have done as a family each year to celebrate holidays and other special occasions. Lisa did just that, and, much to her surprise and my delight, she came into the following class meeting with a journal entry full of activities in which her family engaged on a regular ba-sis. That is, she came into class with a record of family tradi-tions she could explore and discuss in writing. You will have the opportunity to read some of Lisa's work in a later chapter. For now, however, you will find here a number of activities that should help you better recognize the folklore of your own folk. The first of these activities is what I call the Self-Ethno-graphic Questionnaire. Most of the questions, you can answer on your own, but there may be a few that will require you to ask questions of family members or go out into your community to discover the folklore that shapes and surrounds you.

DISCOVERING FOLKLORE

Thinking Ahead

Our families, our communities take many forms. Do you consider your family to be your biological relatives or do you consider your family the friends, teammates, or co-workers with whom you spend your time? Do you consider your community to be the people in your town, your neighbors next door and/or on your block, or the members of a group to which you belong. Before beginning the following exercise, define your family and community.

A Self-Ethnographic Questionnaire

Directions: In your journal, do your best to answer as many of the following questions as you can. If you have trouble answering a question on your own, do research, conduct interviews, or, using your own definition of family or community, simply have discussions with family or community members to help you come to a conclusion. If you can't answer a question, leave it blank for now and come back to it later as your studies of family and community folklore progress.

1. Make a list of the things orally or customarily handed-down in your family or community. For instance, did you learn the story of your grandparent's courtship from your grandmother? Did your best friend teach you how to bead? Did the women in your community show you how to quilt? Did your co-workers pass to you the best chair in the office? Did you learn how to bake bread from your father? How to sew from your mother? Was your mother's engagement ring originally your grandmother's, and was it your grandfather's mother's ring before that? Is it a custom in your family for this ring to be handed down from mother to son to wife?

2. Go through a year in the life of your family or community and make a list of the traditional occasions celebrated by that group.

3. Divide into two categories the list you created for question 2: one category for those traditions common to others (such as the celebration of a religious or national holiday), and another category for those traditions specific to your family or community (such as your family's weekly pizza and movie night, your friends' annual week at the shore, your co-workers' Friday night out on the town, your community's ice cream social, folk festival, canoe race, or fireman's carnival).

4. Which yearly family or community events do you engage in or look forward to? What role do you play? What role do these events play in your life? Can you determine their meaning or purpose?

5. Do you or does anyone in your family/community produce or use folk artifacts such as traditional quilts, baskets, woodwork, or pottery?

6. Is there a storyteller in your family/community? If so, who is it and what stories or types of stories is he/she known to tell?

7. Which family and/or community story or stories do you like best? What purpose(s) does this story (or stories) serve?

8. Is there a story a family or community member tells about you? If so, who is the storyteller and why (under what circumstances, on what occasions) is the story most often told?

9. Why do you think this person tells this story about you? Does that person's telling of the story reflect the relationship the two of you have? Does it suggest or affirm a connection you share?

10. What does the story (of questions 8 and 9) reveal about your personality? What does it conceal or fail to show about your personality, your character?

11. Answer either a or b:

    a. A family's oral tradition often is the way they preserve the history behind nicknames and family sayings. Does anyone in your family have a nickname? Do you know the story behind the nickname? How did you learn it? How is it shared with other family members?

    b. Does your family have a saying or expression that only family members or very close friends understand? What is the saying or expression? What gave rise to the saying or expression and in what situations does your family use it now?

12. Is there a story that circulates in your community surrounding a community member (such as a lady with twenty cats) or a particular place in your community (such as a haunted house)? What is the story?

13. How did you hear the story?

14. In what situations is this story most likely to be told? Do adults or children tell it?

15. Do you know where the story originated? Are there multiple versions of this story? Which is your favorite? Record it here.

16. Does your family or community engage in any rite of passage customs (these are typically those traditions that celebrate or mark births, adolescence, coming of age, courtship, marriage, anniversaries) or customs assembled around work, recreation, or social events (these might include quilting bees, bake-offs, apple peelings, corn shuckings, hay balings and rides, house raisings, or turkey shoots)?

17. Is there an account (called an origin story) of how your family or community came to settle where it did or how the family or community name evolved? If so, record it here.

Helpful hint: If you know there is one, but you don't know it yourself, interview family or community members who know the story and will share it with you. Record the story or stories in your journal.

SHARING FOLKLORE

More than likely, you will find yourself quite familiar with the shape of the next activity, for most of us engage in storytelling on a regular basis. That is, we tell stories almost everyday. Yet there are only a few of these stories that make it into our individual collections of personal narratives—those stories told over and over again about us and/or by us. Why does this happen? This mainly occurs because putting our days in the shape of a story is a natural process; it aids us in making conversation and is an effective means of sharing ourselves with others, of passing the time. In addition, we keep some stories and discard others because only a few of our daily stories prove themselves worthy of retelling—have meaning and purpose beyond the immediate moment and present audience. Even at the ripe old age of thirty-six, I still have only a handful of personal stories that have withstood this test of time and circumstances, ones that I repeatedly tell about myself in order to entertain and educate others. For instance, while I may tell my neighbor about what a great run I had this morning, most likely this story will not become a part of my personal story collection. However, there are two "running stories" I frequently tell to both excite my listener's imagination (because they are scary) and teach listeners a lesson about the dangers of running alone. These are stories my family knows and that my very close friends are able to recite as well, even when I am not present. These are the types of stories I want you to think about as you engage in the following activities.

The Joint Venture: A Storytelling Session

Part I

Journal Activity

Option 1.   See if you can list at least two stories you tell about yourself that you believe will eventually become a part of your collection of personal narratives. Do not write out the stories in their entirety yet. However, for each story on your list, try to determine why the story has been retained, why you feel it is worthy of becoming a part of your collection, what entertainment value it has, and what lesson(s) it contains.

Option 2.   See if you can list at least two or three stories a family/community member tells about him- or herself that you believe are a part of his or her collection of personal narratives. Do not write out the stories in their entirety yet. However, for each story on your list, try to determine why the story has been retained, why it is worthy of being a part of the individual's collection, what entertainment value it has, and what lesson(s) it contains.

Part II

In-Class Sharing

Choose one of the preceding stories to share with the class. Give it a title as a way of introducing it to your classmates, but do not identify or define for your classmates the story's entertainment value or lesson. See if they can determine why the story is told, in what situations and/or under what circumstance it might be told, what its entertainment value is, and what the underlying message is.

Part III Writing Folklore

A Story to Writing Lesson

Now that you have engaged in a storytelling session and determined the meaning behind a number of stories, you are ready to begin writing about stories and storytelling itself. The first thing you must do for this exercise is choose one of the stories from the list you developed for the Journal Activity. Then, choose one of the following options.

Option 1.   Write an essay in which you share the story as well as work to convey the principal reason the story gets told.

Option 2.   Since some of us are more adept at storytelling than others, you may opt to write an essay describing the storyteller in your life, focusing on one particular story this person has shared with you in order to convey the individual's mastery of the storytelling craft. For this essay, describe the storyteller in action and focus both on the lesson of the particular story (why it is told) and on what can be learned from this storyteller about the craft of storytelling itself.

Option 3.   If you consider yourself to be the storyteller in your family, write an essay describing how you learned to tell a story well. Did you learn from someone else's good example—from his or her storytelling talents? Or did you learn by realizing what was missing from or wrong with someone else's storytelling abilities? Using a story you frequently tell, describe the elements you feel are necessary to telling a good story and how you incorporate them into your own storytelling. To help you with this option, you might want to read the **Sample Student Essay** that follows.

Sample Student Essay

Storytelling My Way

JENNIFER WEILER

There is only one thing that thrills me more than hearing a great story being told by a talented storyteller and that is being the person telling a great story. I love watching people's expressions when I have them right where I want them in a story. I feel a rush of success when people laugh at the joke I planted in a story, or when they show surprise at the sudden twist in plot I created by shaping the story just right. I am also thrilled when I see my story has moved my listeners, filled them with an emotion they cannot contain, whether the emotion is sorrow or joy. I never thought about the talent that it takes to tell a story until I found myself frustrated with people who couldn't tell a story to save their lives. For instance, one day while my mother was relating to my brother Ed an incident that had happened to her and me on vacation, I found myself silently critiquing the way my mother was telling the story. I wanted her to get to the funny part and leave out the insignificant details that kept taking her listeners (Ed) and me away from her story's point. At that moment, I realized how much I love telling stories, especially our family stories, and that I am good at it.

It may appear that storytelling comes naturally to people, but this is not always the case. While I was growing up, my brother Ed was always the storyteller in the family and this, I believe, was because he was so charismatic; people were simply drawn to Ed no matter what he did. Now, Ed is a good storyteller, but, just as my mother has a difficulty with storytelling, my brother's storytelling has one major problem: he too much enjoys hearing himself speak. That is, he gets so wrapped up in his own voice that he forgets his listeners are even present. The funny thing is Ed is the one who told me, when I was a little girl, that I could not tell a story. Ed was right. I loved to talk and talk and talk, to the point that my mother often ignored me for hours as I rambled on. I would tell the same story for days if I could, but, like my brother, I had not a care for my listener; they weren't even a part of the experience. Eventually, I began paying attention to how other people told stories and I spent a good deal of time observing those listening to the stories being told. Over time I learned how to read people, how to lure them through a story. That is, when it came to telling a good story and telling it well, I learned how to focus on what my listeners wanted and needed and how to put their wants and needs first. Finally, one summer while I was at camp, all the kids wanted me to tell the stories around the campfire at fun hour. I had a few kids ask me to tell their stories to the rest of the group because they said I was the best storyteller around. That summer I worked at the craft of storytelling, completely open to the idea that storytelling is an art form to be mastered.

When it comes to storytelling, the first thing I try to do is bring the story to the audience as if it has never been told before, as if this is its first time coming out to meet the world. Before I even start a story, however, I have to determine my audience. Do they like to laugh or do they lack humor? Are they sharp and witty? Do they take seriously everything in life? In addition, I have come to know that no matter what personality types make up my audience, most people want a believable story and won't stand for unimaginable details. Once I have my audience identified, then I have to give them my full attention. Many people believe that storytellers love the attention they get and they do, but we rely on our listeners for the attention we crave. Hence, it is a partnership.

A storyteller takes on a big responsibility in relaying a story: to bring a past incident to life and in living color. In this way, the story itself is an entity of its own. The storyteller—me—is just a passageway through which the story travels to reach a new listener and to stay alive. The best passageway, in my opinion, is one that is both old and new. For instance, I have a knack for remembering which story details have worked in the past and which details have failed. I know to bring the effective details back the next time I tell the story and, moreover, to re-shape or discard those that didn't work, depending on to whom and for what reason the story is being told this time. I do this so it seems the story was made for that particular moment and no other. I have found that this is another thing all listeners want—to feel as though the story was made especially for them, which, if a story is done right, becomes the truth anyway.

If I get to know my listeners, the story details are easy to figure out. And as I am relating a story to them, it is not hard to move them right where I want them. This is when I get the "storyteller's rush." Presenting a story and engaging the full attention of one person or ten people is an incredible feeling. My family holiday dinners are remembered for the moment when we begin telling the stories—especially the embarrassing ones—of the adults' childhoods. These storytelling rituals have been taking place in my family since I was a child. Thus, it is not surprising that I have a Rolodex in my head full of great family stories. As the years went on and I became more vocal at family functions, I began to relay the stories I had heard when I was little. Those who had told their stories to me—the stories I was now telling to new family members—began to comment on the fact that they felt I could tell their stories better than they could. And it became my job to do just that—to bring my family's history to life.

I have taken it upon myself to seek out and retain my family's oral history, whether it is the story my grandmother doesn't want told or the story my Uncle Jack will help me tell if he has enough liquor in his belly. Like me, the whole family knows that once our eldest members pass on, the history of our origins goes with them. I don't want to see that happen. I hope that in the future there will be another child in our family like me, a girl or a boy gifted with the art of storytelling, to whom I can pass the tools of my craft, the legacy that is my family's history.

Heirlooms
and Legacies

THE FOLKLORE FOCUS

Family Heirlooms, Family Legacies

According to the compilers of *A Celebration of American Family Folklore* (Zeitlin, Kofkin, and Baker 1982), "While story-telling, picture-taking, and the celebration of other rituals occur on specific occasions, families go about their daily lives surrounded by many objects . . . which stand as silent reminders of their heritage" (200). It is likely that your day-to-day lives reflect the truth of this statement and illustrate that heirlooms—tangible items such as rings, furniture, tool sets—take many shapes. And your interactions with older family and community members probably provide much evidence that our legacies—those intangible aspects of a family's/community's heritage—vary as well. The narrative lessons, examples from experience, and doors to the future our elders share with or open for us hold just as much value as those concrete objects they have lovingly maintained and handed over to us. In other words, both heirlooms and legacies serve an important purpose in our lives. Like all other folklore forms, they have the power to connect us to the past, situate us in the present, and prepare us for the future.

My own experience with heirlooms and legacies attests to the power inherent in these forms of folklore. Before my grandparents moved from the old family home into a small apartment in an assisted living community, they held a family auction so that instead of having family members fight over

11

who got what of their cherished belongings, each of us could get what we wanted if we were willing to pay for it. Now, this may seem a strange way of keeping family treasures in the family, but it worked in the manner my grandparents intended. We did not fight over Grandma's hope chest or the first grandfather clock Grandpa ever made. We were respectful of each other's needs. We knew who liked each item best, and we worked together to ensure each family member got what his or her heart desired. All went home with their cars loaded and their hearts full. Later, we found out that the money we spent on these family belongings went into our trusts to be returned to us on a sadder date. By doing what they did, not only did my grandparents pass on to us a number of precious family heirlooms, but also they conveyed a legacy of behavior that no one in the family will soon forget.

These days I can recall my family's history by simply looking around my home and gazing at the heirlooms that furnish it. There in my bedroom is my grandmother's hope chest, filled still with her wedding quilt and her handmade throw blankets. In my living room, there is the desk my grandfather made for himself when he set out on his own; it houses my bill-paying instruments and his first pair of reading glasses. And tying together these and the many other heirlooms that grace my home is the memory of one of the most important lessons my grandparents ever taught me: when families work together, each member benefits. Like the history-filled furniture I own (my grandparents' heirlooms), this way of thinking (my grandparents' legacy) is a part of who I am. Both are aspects of my heritage I plan to pass on to my own children.

What objects, what modes of behavior have been passed to you? Which ones would you like to convey to the next generation? This chapter encourages you to think carefully about the heirlooms and legacies that shape your life. The readings selected for this chapter and the questions that follow them will help you do this. Each selection highlights the significance of a particular heirloom and/or legacy, and together, they illustrate the various forms these aspects of heritage can take. The questions that follow each selection require you to further analyze the readings, not only to study the various forms heirlooms and legacies take, but to compare the purposes they serve and the ways they are viewed. As you study the selections themselves and compare them to each other, make note of the way the writers use sensory details to convey the emotion and meaning of the heirloom(s) or legacy(ies) at the heart of their works. In your memories of and experiences with heirlooms and legacies, you have an ample supply of meaningful writing material. Your study of the precise detailing necessary to accurately describe heirlooms and legacies in writing will prepare you to practice sensory detailing when it is your turn to write more fully about those things handed down to you from the preceding generations—those things you, too, might like to pass on.

The Grammar of Silk
Cathy Song

Born (1955) and raised in Honolulu, Hawaii, Cathy Song is the author of a number of collections of poetry and the recipient of the 1982 Yale Series of Younger Poets Award. Her publications include *Picture Bride; Frameless Windows, Squares of Light; School Figures;* and *The Lord of Bliss*.

My Thoughts in Writing

1. Although Song's poem certainly reflects her Asian cultural heritage, this does not seem to be the primary cultural group depicted in the poem. On which specific cultural group does the speaker focus? What lines support your answer?
2. In the poem, the speaker tells us that her mother was "determined that I should sew / as if she knew what she herself was missing." According to the speaker, what was the mother missing? How does what the mother lacked affect the daughter's view of what she was forced to learn?
3. This poem strives to convey a sense of tradition. What is the tradition being passed from mother to daughter in this poem? According to the speaker, what are the essential elements of this tradition and how will it become an es-

sential in her own life? Is the tradition an heirloom or a
legacy? How do you know?

————————— ✦ —————————

On Saturdays in the morning
my mother sent me to Mrs. Umemoto's sewing school.
It was cool and airy in her basement,
pleasant—a word I choose
to use years later to describe   5
the long tables where we sat
and cut, pinned, and stitched,
the Singer's companionable whirr,
the crisp, clever bite of scissors
parting like silver fish a river of calico.   10

The school was in walking distance
to Kaimuki Dry Goods
where my mother purchased my supplies—
small cards of buttons,
zippers and rickrack packaged like licorice,   15
lifesaver rolls of thread
in fifty-yard lengths,
spun from spools, tough as tackle.
Seamstresses waited at the counters
like librarians to be consulted.   20
Pens and scissors dangled like awkward pendants
across flat chests,
a scarf of measuring tape flung across a shoulder,
time as a pincushion bristled at the wrist.
They deciphered a dress's blueprints   25
with an architect's keen eye.

This evidently was a sanctuary,
a place where women confined with children
conferred, consulted the oracle,
the stone tablets of the latest pattern books.   30
Here mothers and daughters paused in symmetry,
offered the proper reverence—
hushed murmurings for the shantung silk
which required a certain sigh,
as if it were a piece from the Ming Dynasty.   35

My mother knew there would be no shortcuts
and headed for the remnants,
the leftover bundles with yardage
enough for a heart-shaped pillow,
a child's dirndl, a blouse without darts.   40
Along the aisles
my fingertips touched the titles—
satin, tulle, velvet,
peach, lavender, pistachio,
sherbet-colored linings—   45
and settled for the plain brown-and-white composition
of polka dots on kettle cloth
my mother held up in triumph.

She was determined that I should sew
as if she knew what she herself was missing,   50
a moment when she could have come up for air—
the children asleep,
the dishes drying on the rack—
and turned on the lamp
and pulled back the curtain of sleep.   55
To inhabit the night,
the night as a black cloth, white paper,
a sheet of music in which she might find herself singing.

On Saturdays at Mrs. Umemoto's sewing school,
when I took my place beside the other girls,   60
bent my head and went to work,
my foot keeping time on the pedal,
it was to learn the charitable oblivion
of hand and mind as one—
a refuge such music affords the maker—   65
the pleasure of notes in perfectly measured time.

Heritage

Linda Hogan

Linda Hogan was born in Denver, Colorado, in 1947. Her published works, which typically reflect her Chickasaw heritage,
include poems, stories, screenplays, essays, and novels. She is

a recipient of an American Book Award, a Colorado Book Award, and a Pulitzer nomination. She currently teaches creative writing at the University of Colorado at Boulder.

My Thoughts in Writing

1. This poem contains a list of the things the speaker received from the members of her family. What kinds of items make up this list? What is the speaker's attitude toward each item? How do you know?

2. What particular aspects of her cultural heritage does the speaker recall and record in writing? Why might it be important to her that she does such culturally specific recollecting? In the end, what is the speaker's attitude toward her family heirlooms and legacies? Is it positive or negative? How do you know?

3. Study the list you created for question 1 and then decide which items are heirlooms and which are legacies. Compare and contrast the lists. How do the items on the legacy list differ from each other? What can you conclude from this?

———————— ✦ ————————

From my mother, the antique mirror
where I watch my face take on her lines.
She left me the smell of baking bread
to warm fine hairs in my nostrils,
she left the large white breasts that weigh down   5
my body.

From my father I take his brown eyes,
the plague of locusts that leveled our crops,
they flew in formation like buzzards.

From my uncle the whittled wood   10
that rattles like bones
and is white
and smells like all our old houses
that are no longer there. He was the man
who sang old chants to me, the words   15
my father was told not to remember.

From my grandfather who never spoke
I learned to fear silence.

I learned to kill a snake
when you're begging for rain.   20

And Grandmother, blue-eyed woman
whose skin was brown,
she used snuff.
When her coffee can full of black saliva
spilled on me   25
it was like the brown cloud of grasshoppers
that leveled her fields.
It was the brown stain
that covered my white shirt,
my whiteness a shame.   30
That sweet black liquid like the food
she chewed up and spit into my father's mouth
when he was an infant.
It was the brown earth of Oklahoma
stained with oil.   35
She said tobacco would purge your body of poisons.
It has more medicine than stones and knives
against your enemies.
That tobacco is the dark night that covers me.

She said it is wise to eat the flesh of deer   40
so you will be swift and travel over many miles.
She told me how our tribe has always followed a stick
that pointed west
that pointed east.
From my family I have learned the secrets   45
of never having a home.

Inspired Eccentricity
bell hooks

bell hooks, born Gloria Jean Watkins in 1952, is a teacher, writer, and social critic whose published works reflect her concern for the ways race, class, and gender intersect. She has taught literature, women's studies, and African American studies at Yale University, Oberlin College, and City College of New York.

My Thoughts in Writing

1. hooks begins her essay by speaking directly to you, the reader. Her statement that "there are family members you try to forget and ones that you always remember, that you can't stop talking about" is purposeful. Why do you think she begins her essay this way? How effective is this kind of beginning?

2. In paragraph three, hooks writes that Baba and Daddy Gus gave her a "worldview that sustained [her] during a difficult and painful childhood." How might an elder's worldview become a legacy capable of sustaining members of the next generations?

3. Study hooks's essay carefully. Where does hooks first identify the elements of the legacy her grandparents gave her? What makes up this legacy? In the essay's final paragraph, hooks lists a number of family heirlooms she cherishes. How are these heirlooms similar to the legacy Baba and Daddy Gus left her? Why do you think this similarity is highlighted in the end?

✦

There are family members you try to forget and ones that you always remember, that you can't stop talking about. They may be dead—long gone—but their presence lingers and you have to share who they were and who they still are with the world. You want everyone to know them as you did, to love them as you did.

All my life I have remained enchanted by the presence of my mother's parents, Sarah and Gus Oldham. When I was a child they were already old. I did not see that then, though. They were Baba and Daddy Gus, together for more than seventy years at the time of his death. Their marriage fascinated me. They were strangers and lovers—two eccentrics who created their own world.

More than any other family members, together they gave me a worldview that sustained me during a difficult and painful childhood. Reflecting on the eclectic writer I have become, I see in myself a mixture of these two very different but equally powerful figures from my childhood. Baba was tall, her skin so white and her hair so jet black and straight that she could have easily "passed" denying all traces of blackness. Yet the man she married was short and dark, and sometimes his skin looked like the color of soot from burning coal. In our childhood the fireplaces burned coal. It was bright heat, luminous and fierce. If you got too close it could burn you.

Together Baba and Daddy Gus generated a hot heat. He was a man of few words, deeply committed to silence—so much so that it was like a religion to him. When he spoke you could hardly hear what he said. Baba was just the opposite. Smoking an abundance of cigarettes a day, she talked endlessly. She preached. She yelled. She fussed. Often her vitriolic rage would heap itself on Daddy Gus, who would sit calmly in his chair by the stove, as calm and still as the Buddha sits. And when he had enough of her words, he would reach for his hat and walk.

Neither Baba nor Daddy Gus drove cars. Rarely did they   5
ride in them. They preferred walking. And even then their styles were different. He moved slow, as though carrying a great weight; she with her tall, lean, boyish frame moved swiftly, as though there was never time to waste. Their one agreed-upon passion was fishing. Though they did not do even that together. They lived close but they created separate worlds.

In a big two-story wood frame house with lots of rooms they constructed a world that could contain their separate and distinct personalities. As children one of the first things we noticed about our grandparents was that they did not sleep in the same room. This arrangement was contrary to everything we understood about marriage. While Mama never wanted to talk about their separate worlds, Baba would tell you in a minute that Daddy Gus was nasty, that he smelled like tobacco juice, that he did not wash enough, that there was no way she would want him in her bed. And while he would say nothing nasty about her, he would merely say why would he want to share somebody else's bed when he could have his own bed to himself, with no one to complain about anything.

I loved my granddaddy's smells. Always, they filled my nostrils with the scent of happiness. It was sheer ecstasy for me to be allowed into his inner sanctum. His room was a small Van Gogh–like space off from the living room. There was no door. Old-fashioned curtains were the only attempt at privacy. Usually the curtains were closed. His room reeked of tobacco. There were treasures everywhere in that small room. As a younger man Daddy Gus did odd jobs, and sometimes even in his old age he would do a chore for some needy lady. As he went about his work, he would pick up found objects, scraps. All these objects would lie about his room, on the dresser, on the table near his bed. Unlike all other grown-ups he never cared about children looking through his things. Anything we wanted he gave to us.

Daddy Gus collected beautiful wooden cigar boxes. They held lots of the important stuff—the treasures. He had tons of little diaries that he made notes in. He gave me my first wallet, my first teeny little book to write in, my first beautiful pen, which did not write for long, but it was still a found and shared treasure. When I would lie on his bed or sit close to him, sometimes just standing near, I would feel all the pain and anxiety of my troubled childhood leave me. His spirit was calm. He gave me the unconditional love I longed for.

"Too calm," his grown-up children thought. That's why he had let this old woman rule him, my cousin BoBo would say. Even as children we knew that grown-ups felt sorry for Daddy Gus. At times his sons seemed to look upon him as not a "real man." His refusal to fight in wars was another sign to them of weakness. It was my grandfather who taught me to oppose war. They saw him as a man controlled by the whims of others, by this tall, strident, demanding woman he had married. I saw him as a man of profound beliefs, a man of integrity. When he heard their put-downs—for they talked on and on about his laziness—he merely muttered that he had no use for them. He was not gonna let anybody tell him what to do with his life.

10   Daddy Gus was a devout believer, a deacon at his church; he was one of the right-hand men of God. At church, everyone admired his calmness. Baba had no use for church. She liked nothing better than to tell us all the ways it was one big hypocritical place: "Why, I can find God anywhere I want to—I do

not need a church." Indeed, when my grandmother died, her funeral could not take place in a church, for she had never belonged. Her refusal to attend church bothered some of her daughters, for they thought she was sinning against God, setting a bad example for the children. We were not supposed to listen when she began to damn the church and everybody in it.

Baba loved to "cuss." There was no bad word she was not willing to say. The improvisational manner in which she would string those words together was awesome. It was the goddamn sons of bitches who thought that they could fuck with her when they could just kiss her black ass. A woman of strong words and powerful metaphors, she could not read or write. She lived in the power of language. Her favorite sayings were a prelude for storytelling. It was she who told me, "Play with a puppy, he'll lick you in the mouth." When I heard this saying, I knew what was coming—a long polemic about not letting folks get too close, 'cause they will mess with you.

Baba loved to tell her stories. And I loved to hear them. She called me Glory. And in the midst of her storytelling she would pause to say, "Glory, are ya listenin'. Do you understand what I'm telling ya." Sometimes I would have to repeat the lessons I had learned. Sometimes I was not able to get it right and she would start again. When Mama felt I was learning too much craziness "over home" (that is what we called Baba's house), my visits were curtailed. As I moved into my teens I learned to keep to myself all the wisdom of the old ways I picked up over home.

Baba was an incredible quilt maker, but by the time I was old enough to really understand her work; to see its beauty; she was already having difficulty with her eyesight. She could not sew as much as in the old days, when her work was on everybody's bed. Unwilling to throw anything away, she loved to make crazy quilts, 'cause they allowed every scrap to be used. Although she would one day order patterns and make perfect quilts with colors that went together, she always collected scraps.

Long before I read Virginia Woolf's *A Room of One's Own* I learned from Baba that a woman needed her own space to work. She had a huge room for her quilting. Like every other space in the private world she created upstairs, it had her treasures, an endless array of hatboxes, feathers, and trunks filled with old clothes she had held on to. In room after room there were feather tick mattresses; when they were pulled back, the wooden slats of the bed were revealed, lined with exquisite hand-sewn quilts.

15   In all these trunks, in crevices and drawers were braided tobacco leaves to keep away moths and other insects. A really hot summer could make cloth sweat, and stains from tobacco juice would end up on quilts no one had ever used. When I was a young child, a quilt my grandmother had made kept me warm, was my solace and comfort. Even though Mama protested when I dragged that old raggedy quilt from Kentucky to Stanford, I knew I needed that bit of the South, of Baba's world, to sustain me.

Like Daddy Gus, she was a woman of her word. She liked to declare with pride, "I mean what I say and I say what I mean." "Glory," she would tell me, "nobody is better than their word—if you can't keep ya word you ain't worth nothin' in this world." She would stop speaking to folk over the breaking of their word, over lies. Our mama was not given to loud speech or confrontation. I learned all those things from Baba—"to stand up and speak up" and not to "give a good goddamn" what folk who "ain't got a pot to pee in" think. My parents were concerned with their image in the world. It was pure blasphemy for Baba to teach that it did not matter what other folks thought—"Ya have to be right with yaself in ya own heart—that's all that matters." Baba taught me to listen to my heart—to follow it. From her we learned as small children to remember our dreams in the night and to share them when we awakened. They would be interpreted by her. She taught us to listen to the knowledge in dreams. Mama would say this was all nonsense, but she too was known to ask the meaning of a dream.

In their own way my grandparents were rebels, deeply committed to radical individualism. I learned how to be myself from them. Mama hated this. She thought it was important to be liked, to conform. She had hated growing up in such an eccentric, otherworldly household. This world where folks made their own wine, their own butter, their own soap; where chickens were raised, and huge gardens were grown for canning everything. This was the world Mama wanted to leave behind. She wanted store-bought things.

Baba lived in another time, a time when all things were produced in the individual household. Everything the family needed was made at home. She loved to tell me stories about learning to trap animals, to skin, to soak possum and coon in brine, to fry up a fresh rabbit. Though a total woman of the outdoors who could shoot and trap as good as any man, she still believed every woman should sew—she made her first quilt as a girl. In her world, women were as strong as men because they had to be. She had grown up in the country and knew that country ways were the best ways to live. Boasting about being able to do anything that a man could do and better, this woman who could not read or write was confident about her place in the universe.

My sense of aesthetics came from her. She taught me to really look at things, to see underneath the surface, to see the different shades of red in the peppers she had dried and hung in the kitchen sunlight. The beauty of the ordinary, the everyday, was her feast of light. While she had no use for the treasures in my granddaddy's world, he too taught me to look for the living spirit in things—the things that are cast away but still, need to be touched and cared for. Picking up a found object he would tell me its story or tell me how he was planning to give it life again.

Connected in spirit but so far apart in the life of everyday-ness, Baba and Daddy Gus were rarely civil to each other. Every shared talk begun with goodwill ended in disagreement and contestation. Everyone knew Baba just loved to fuss. She liked a good war of words. And she was comfortable using words to sting and hurt, to punish. When words would not do the job, she could reach for the strap, a long piece of black leather that would leave tiny imprints on the flesh.

There was no violence in Daddy Gus. Mama shared that he had always been that way, a calm and gentle man, full of tenderness: I remember clinging to his tenderness when nothing I did was right in my mother's eyes, when I was constantly

punished. Baba was not an ally. She advocated harsh punishment. She had no use for children who would not obey. She
was never ever affectionate. When we entered her house, we
gave her a kiss in greeting and that was it. With Daddy Gus we
could cuddle, linger in his arms, give as many kisses as desired. His arms and heart were always open.

In the back of their house were fruit trees, chicken coops,
and gardens, and in the front were flowers. Baba could make
anything grow. And she knew all about herbs and roots. Her
home remedies healed our childhood sicknesses. Of course
she thought it crazy for anyone to go to a doctor when she
could tell them just what they needed. All these things she had
learned from her mother, Bell Blair Hooks, whose name I
would choose as my pen name. Everyone agreed that I had the
temperament of this great-grandmother I would not remember. She was a sharp-tongued woman. Or so they said. And it
was believed I had inherited my way with words from her.

Families do that. They chart psychic genealogies that often overlook what is right before our eyes. I may have inherited my great-grandmother Bell Hook's way with words, but I
learned to use those words listening to my grandmother. I
learned to be courageous by seeing her act without fear. I
learned to risk because she was daring. Home and family were
her world. While my grandfather journeyed downtown, visited
at other folks' houses, went to church, and conducted affairs
in the world, Baba rarely left home. There was nothing in the
world she needed. Things out there violated her spirit.

As a child I had no sense of what it would mean to live a
life, spanning so many generations, unable to read or write. To
me Baba was a woman of power. That she would have been
extraordinarily powerless in a world beyond 1200 Broad
Street was a thought that never entered my mind. I believed
that she stayed home because it was the place she liked best.
Just as Daddy Gus seemed to need to walk—to roam.

25   After his death it was easier to see the ways that they complemented and completed each other. For suddenly, without
him as a silent backdrop, Baba's spirit was diminished. Something in her was forever lonely and could not find solace.
When she died, tulips, her favorite flower, surrounded her. The

preacher told us that her death was not an occasion for grief, for "it is hard to live in a world where your choicest friends are gone." Daddy Gus was the companion she missed most. His presence had always been the mirror of memory. Without it there was so much that could not be shared. There was no witness.

Seeing their life together, I learned that it was possible for women and men to fashion households arranged around their own needs. Power was shared. When there was an imbalance, Baba ruled the day. It seemed utterly alien to me to learn about black women and men not making families and homes together. I had not been raised in a world of absent men. One day I knew I would fashion a life using the patterns I inherited from Baba and Daddy Gus. I keep treasures in my cigar box, which still smells after all these years. The quilt that covered me as a child remains, full of ink stains and faded colors. In my trunks are braided tobacco leaves, taken from over home. They keep evil away—keep bad spirits from crossing the threshold, like the ancestors they guard and protect.

Walking in Lucky Shoes
BETTE BAO LORD

Bette Bao Lord, born in Shanghai, China, in 1938, immigrated to the United States in 1946. She attended Tufts University and won the American Book Award for her first novel, *Spring Moon* (1982). She works in fiction and nonfiction and created the following selection as a piece for *Newsweek* magazine's guest editorial column.

My Thoughts in Writing

1. In paragraph two, Lord writes, "At 8, I sailed for American from Shanghai without a passing acquaintance of A, B or C, wearing scruffy brown oxfords. Little did I know then that they were as magical as those glittering red pumps that propelled Dorothy down the yellow brick road." What

made Lord's brown oxfords so special? How do you know? Use the text to illustrate your point?

2. Make a list of the types of shoes Lord mentions in the essay. How are her shoes related to the situations she remembers? What do all these shoes have to do with her main point?

3. In conclusion, Lord mentions the legacy her essay highlights and reflects. What is that legacy? What type of legacy is it? How does Lord's essay serve to pass on this legacy?

———————— ✦ ————————

I confess, Novelists have a fetish. We can't resist shoes. Indeed, we spend our lives recalling the pairs we have shed and snatching others off unsuspecting souls. We're not proud. We're not particular. Whether it's Air Jordans or the clodhoppers of Frankenstein, Imelda's gross collection or one glass slipper, we covet them all. There's no cure for this affliction. To create characters, we must traipse around and around in our heads sporting lost or stolen shoes.

At 8, I sailed for America from Shanghai without a passing acquaintance of A, B or C, wearing scruffy brown oxfords. Little did I know then that they were as magical as those glittering red pumps that propelled Dorothy down the yellow brick road.

Only yesterday, it seems, resting my chin on the rails of the SS *Marylinx*, I peered into the mist for *Mei Guo*, Beautiful Country. It refused to appear. Then, in a blink, there was the Golden Gate, more like the portals to Heaven than the arches of a man-made bridge.

Only yesterday, standing at PS 8 in Brooklyn, I was bewitched—others, alas, were bothered and bewildered—when I proclaimed:

> I pledge a lesson to the frog of
> the United States of America.
> And to the wee puppet for witch's hands.
> One Asian, in the vestibule,
> with little tea and just rice for all.

Although I mangled the language, the message was not   5
lost. Not on someone wearing immigrant shoes.

Only yesterday, rounding third base in galoshes, I swallowed a barrelful of tears wondering what wrong I had committed to anger my teammates so. Why were they all madly screaming at me to go home, go home?

Only yesterday, listening in pink cotton mules to Red Barber broadcasting from Ebbetts Field, I vaulted over the Milky Way as my hero, Jackie Robinson, stole home.

Only yesterday, enduring the pinch of new Mary Janes at my grammar-school graduation, I felt as tall as the Statue of Liberty, reciting Walt Whitman: "I hear America singing, the varied carols I hear. . . . Each singing what belongs to him or her and to none else. . . ."

Today I cherish every unstylish pair of shoes that took me up a road cleared by the footfalls of millions of immigrants before me—to a room of my own. For America has granted me many a dream, even one that I never dared to dream—returning to the land of my birth in 1989 as the wife of the American ambassador. Citizens of Beijing were astounded to see that I was not a *yang guei ze*, foreign devil, with a tall nose and ghostly skin and bumpy hair colored in outlandish hues, I looked Chinese, I spoke Chinese, and after being in my company they accused me of being a fake, of being just another member of the clan.

I do not believe that the loss of one's native culture is the   10
price one must pay for becoming an American. On the contrary, I feel doubly blessed. I can choose from two rich cultures those parts that suit my mood or the occasion best. And unbelievable as it may seem, shoes tinted red, white and blue go dandy with them all.

Recently I spoke at my alma mater. There were many more Asian faces in that one audience than there were enrolled at Tufts University when I cavorted in white suede shoes to cheer the Jumbos to victory. One asked, "Will you tell us about your encounters with racial prejudice?" I had no ready answers. I thought hard. Sure, I had been roughed up at school. Sure, I had failed at work. Sure, I had at times felt powerless. But had prejudice against the shade of my skin and the shape of my eyes caused these woes? Unable to show off the wounds I had endured at the hands of racists, I could only cite a scene from my husband's 25th reunion at Yale eight years ago. Throughout that weekend, I sensed I was being watched. But even after the tall, burly man finally introduced himself, I did not recognize his face or name. He hemmed and hawed, then announced that he had flown from Colorado to apologize to me. I could not imagine why. Apparently at a party in the early '60s, he had hectored me to cease dating his WASP classmate.

Someone else at Tufts asked, "How do you think of yourself? As a Chinese or as an American?" Without thinking, I blurted out the truth: "Bette Bao Lord." Did I imagine the collective sigh of relief that swept through the auditorium? I think not. Perhaps I am the exception that proves the rule. Perhaps I am blind to insult and injury. Perhaps I am not alone. No doubt I have been lucky. Others have not been as fortunate. They had little choice but to wear ill-fitting shoes warped by prejudice, to start down a less traveled road strewn, with broken promises and littered with regrets, haunted by racism and awash with tears. Where could that road possibly lead? Nowhere but to a nation, divided, without liberty and no justice at all.

The Berlin wall is down, but between East Harlem and West Hempstead, between the huddled masses of yesterday and today, the walls go up and up. Has the cold war ended abroad only to usher in heated racial and tribal conflicts at home? No, I believe we shall overcome. But only when:

We engage our diversity to yield a nation greater than the sum of its parts.

15   We can be different as sisters and brothers are, and belong to the same family.

We bless, not shame, America, our home.

A home, no doubt, where skeletons nest in closets and the roof leaks, where foundations must be shored and rooms added. But a home where legacies conceived by the forefathers are tendered from generation to generation to have and to hold. Legacies not of gold but as intangible and inalienable and invaluable as laughter and hope.

We the people can do just that—if we clear the smoke of ethnic chauvinism and fears by braving our journey to that "City Upon a Hill" in each other's shoes.

Sample Student Essay

My Great-Grandfather's Shaving Brush

Howard Bennett

Most people would think it is nothing more than a scrawny old shaving brush, but it has been passed down in my family from father to eldest son for at least four generations. It is a small shaving brush, about three inches high and one inch in diameter, with a stained ivory handle. The brush's few remaining hairs are from a badger; all good shaving brushes are made of badger hair. While it has no monetary value, it establishes a connection with my past, and, therefore, it is priceless.

I never met my father's father. He and my father's mother died before I was born. I was married and living in Germany, as a member of the United States Armed Forces, when my own father suddenly died. I could not leave my pregnant wife to attend his funeral, for it was a bad time for her to travel. Shortly after the funeral, my mother sent me several small items that were important to my dad. The shaving brush was among those items.

Today, most of the stuff my mother sent me is gone. I kept the cheap pocketknife for a while. And, before I finally gave up trying to keep it running, I spent many dollars upkeeping my dad's Bulova wristwatch. After that, it stayed in a bureau drawer until it simply disappeared among my socks. I still have a few of the Canadian coins my dad kept from the booze-smuggling trips he and my mother took to Canada during the prohibition era. My dad told me that Customs caught him and my mother as often as not. The penalty was confiscation and destruction of the prohibited bottles but, according to my dad, understanding Customs agents would frequently overlook a bottle or two.

My dad cherished all of these things, but the pièce de résistance to me was the shaving brush. Dad carefully preserved this precious item by wrapping it in the same cloth bag it had been in when his father gave it to him. My dad had shown me the brush many times, using it as a trigger to tell me stories of his childhood. Perhaps it is not so odd that I wound up telling quite similar stories to my sons whenever the brush came out and I had their attention. As my dad told me, I told my sons about fighting my way to school through snowdrifts that towered over my head; about the girl I fell in love with in the first grade; about being chased by the police for what I thought was a minor infraction.

The brush was supposed to have been of German manufacture, but any identifying marks had long since been worn into illegibility. My father told me that his father, a first-generation American born a few years after his own parents came here from Germany, got the brush from my great-grandfather shortly before he died.

Because of its far-reaching heritage, the brush became a kind of talisman in my family. We could not put a finger on its powers, but we knew that the owner should never get too far from it. We don't know much about what Great-grandfather did with it, but my dad said his father took it with him on trips. I suggested that maybe my grandfather took it with him because he needed something to shave with, but Dad said that his father had a fulsome beard. In other words, my grandfather's reasons for keeping the brush close at hand when far away from home had little to do with shaving. My father followed suit, taking the brush with him whenever he went away, using it for luck rather than for maintaining a close shave. He took the brush with him when he went to Canada to purchase liquor or to Hot Springs, Arkansas, for medicinal baths. I, like the Bennett men before me, kept it close by in the service and it was in my pocket when, while in Munich, my wife gave birth to our first son. "It can't hurt to have it with me." I remember thinking this when I took it along with me to the hospital when my wife gave birth to our second son. Strange as it may sound to you, there is a part of me that believes our sons turned out fine because I had the family shaving brush with me when they were born.

I never shaved with the heirloom brush, nor did my father. Its usefulness for shaving had long since passed when it was handed down to my father. It had so few bristles when it got to me that it could no longer hold water or lather. Still, I remember how good it felt in my hand.

I no longer have the brush. I wanted personally to give it to my eldest son instead of having it passed down to him after my death. It felt a little like the changing of the guard when I gave the cherished brush to my son; both of us had tears in our eyes. I know that my son will preserve our family heirloom until it is time for him to hand it down to his son. I know that my son will tell his children many stories of the brush and where it has been. It is amazing to me how something so mundane can have so much significance, but the shaving brush is worth more to my family than are our expensive cars and houses. They are replaceable; the brush and the memories it contains are not.

My Thoughts in Writing

1. In the first paragraph, Bennett remarks that his family's precious heirloom would be nothing more than a shaving brush to most people. Why is the shaving brush valuable only to the Bennett family, specifically to the Bennett men? Where in the essay does Bennett give the shaving brush meaning beyond its practical use? What is the meaning he gives the brush?

2. Why was it important to Bennett that he give his son the brush before his own death? Do you believe heirlooms should be passed from one generation to the next while the members of both generations are living? Use the essay and your personal experience to explain your answer.

3. Why do you think Bennett tells us about the other items left to him by his father? How valuable were these items? What made the shaving brush the pièce de résistance?

The Readings Come Together

1. Compare the sensory detailing in the essays and the poems. How do the different genres affect the way the details are presented to readers? Does one genre lend itself to descriptive detailing more than the other does? Why or why not? Use specific words, lines, and phrases from the essays and the poems to explain your point.

2. Consider the following elements as you compare and contrast Hogan's poem, "Heritage," and Song's poem, "The Grammar of Silk": the tone of each speaker, the perspective from which the poem is told, how the speaker's point of view affects what is remembered and how it is remembered, the structure of the poems, how structure affects meaning, the attitude the speakers convey toward their legacies, the message each speaker seems to be sending about legacies.

3. Song and hooks describe particular places in relation to the people and legacies they are remembering. Find the similarities shared among the place descriptions in the following list. What might the writers be trying to convey about the relationship between people and places? What does place have to do with the legacy the speakers comment on in each selection? Does place play the same role, have the same purpose, share the same value? Explain your answer.

   - Song's description of the "sanctuary" that was Kaimuki Dry Goods
   - hooks's description of her Daddy Gus's "inner sanctum" (par. 7–8)
   - Baba's "own space to work" (par. 14)

4. Both hooks and Hogan mention heirlooms handed down in their families. Make a list of the heirlooms mentioned in each piece. Then, determine how the heirlooms are viewed in each piece. Are they or are they not viewed in the same way? If they are viewed in the same way, what is the combined message about heirlooms? If they are viewed differently, how do you account for the difference and what is the effect?

5. Although Song and Hogan use detail differently, how does each poet create a vision for the reader? Is one more effective than the other? Use the text to explain and support your answer.

6. Both Lord's and Hogan's works refer to intangible legacies. Compare and contrast the legacies described by Lord and Hogan. Is a similar message conveyed regarding this type of legacy? If so, what is that message? If not, how do the messages differ?

7. Although hooks writes primarily about a legacy, she does discuss heirlooms in her essay. How are the heirlooms mentioned in hooks's essay similar to the shaving brush Bennett writes about? Do the essays convey a similar message about heirlooms? If so, what is that message? If not, how do their messages about heirlooms differ?

There's Something More out There

Part I

At-Home Activity

Option 1. Interview family/community members about the heirlooms in your family/community—those that were handed down to them already, those they would like to have in the future, or personal items that they plan to make heirlooms. As you interview each person, write down the questions that you ask them. In addition, not only should you jot down as much of each answer as you can, you should, if possible, tape-record the entire interview.

Option 2. Interview family/community members about the legacies in your family/community—those that were handed down to them already, those they hope will be passed on, or those in the making. As you interview each person, write down the questions that you ask. In addition, not only should you jot down as much of each answer as you can, you should, if possible, tape-record the entire interview.

Part II

Classroom Storytelling Session

Share family and community heirloom/legacy stories. Get together with two or three of your classmates and share your family/community heirloom and legacy stories. Discuss how they compare and contrast. Choose one of your group's stories to share with the class.

Part III

Journal Entry

Describe your family/community heirloom/legacy—an item such as the shaving brush in Bennett's essay or a legacy of behavior as in "Inspired Eccentricity" by bell hooks, for instance. Focus on creating details that convey the concrete and the abstract aspects of the object or behavior in question.

Part IV

Writing Assignment

Write an essay describing a family/community heirloom or a legacy. Your introduction should make clear your specific purpose for writing. Whether your heirloom/legacy is an item or a mode of behavior, your purpose will be one of the following: to convey through sensory details the heirloom's/legacy's relevance to its original owner, the heirloom's/legacy's relevance to subsequent owner(s), or the heirloom's/legacy's relevance to both its original owner and subsequent owner(s).

CHAPTER 3

Stories and Storytellers

THE FOLKLORE FOCUS

Preserving Family and Community History Through Story

You should already be familiar with this chapter's folklore focus: storytelling. Not only was it a part of your work in the section entitled "Sharing Folklore" in Chapter 1 and a key issue in the sample student essay of that same chapter, but, whether you realize it or not, storytelling is a central element of your everyday lives. In fact, this type of folklore is such a common aspect of most of our lives that we pay very little, if any, attention to the actual role it plays. That is to say, we fail to recognize storytelling as one of our primary means of communication—one of our chief ways of engaging others and making ourselves known. Yet, it is through story that we forge relationships, define our values, and illustrate our unique personalities. Storytelling can also help us and those we share our stories with remember and learn from the past. In some families, like my own, storytelling is the only way the family's history and the lessons learned from those past experiences are maintained from generation to generation. And in some communities, although the facts of the past may be documented in a book of records, the life of that past and its relevance to the present are related only through story.

Telling the Stories of the Stories We Tell

Why do we save some memories to story and discard so many others? Why are some stories told only on Christmas Eve while others are brought out whenever the situation dictates? Our reasons both for telling the stories we tell and for telling those stories when we do are stories in themselves. In other words, there is a story behind every story, and these stories can be just as interesting as the stories to which they refer. It all depends on how well you tell a story in the first place.

Spoken or Written, It Takes Skill to Tell a Good Story

In general, storytelling comes so naturally to us that we have come to see it as simply what we do, a part of human nature, so to speak. Yet, while most of us love to tell our stories and love a good story told to us, few of us are actually good storytellers. Why? Because, as the author of the student essay in Chapter 1 emphasizes, storytelling is an art, a craft to be honed. Think about it. When was the last time you were told a good story? Not a fairy tale, mind you, or a fictional narrative, but a story about an occurrence in someone else's life? More than likely, what made this a good story was a combination of the actual events recounted (the story itself) and the way the teller went about recounting those events (the storytelling). Because our busy, fast-paced lifestyle seems to make our attention spans shorter, most good storytellers will admit that these days, especially, it takes some serious storytelling acrobatics to maintain a listener's interest for any length of time beyond, say, a few minutes. A good storyteller must be able to recall important details, decide which ones matter on the occasion of the story's telling, and work to bring those details to life through careful word choice, fine descriptions, and tonal variations. Good storytellers are in tune with their listeners' needs and expectations, attentive to their reactions, and aware of their level of interest as the story is told. All of this adds up to quite a bit of work on the storyteller's part—but the positive way people respond to a well-told story is also well worth the effort put into getting it right. Moreover, since virtually everyone loves a good story, most love a good storyteller. In other words, a good storyteller is often a fairly popular guy or gal.

How does your family or community use storytelling to preserve history, to influence the present, to shape the future?

How do you use story to communicate with others? Who are the storytellers in your life? This chapter encourages you to think carefully about the role storytelling plays in your life. The readings selected for this chapter and the questions that follow them will help you do this. Each selection highlights the significance of storytelling and of those who tell stories well. Together, they illustrate the value of this form of folklore. The questions that follow each selection require you to further analyze the readings, to not only study storytelling in depth, but to compare the purposes it serves and the ways it is viewed. As you study the selections and compare them to each other, make note of the way the writers use sensory details to convey the way they feel about the folklore and folkloric situations they recall. Written narratives and spoken stories share a similar goal (to convey a central point) and utilize the same techniques (such as action, dialogue, pacing, suspense, vivid sensory detailing, narrative commentary) to create immediacy and a sense of reality for the audience. The narrators of both spoken and written texts want their "listeners" to feel as though they are there in the story, as though what is being described actually happened. Your analysis of each reading's theme (the meaning of the story) and your study of the techniques used to bring a story to life will prepare you to create powerful narratives yourself—to tell and write compelling stories when it is your turn to share your own life experiences with others.

Father Stories

John Edgar Wideman

John Edgar Wideman (born 1941) writes short stories, essays, and novels and has received numerous awards for his work, including the PEN/Faulkner Award for Fiction and the John Dos Passos Prize for Literature. He received degrees from the University of Pennsylvania and Oxford University, where he was a Rhodes Scholar. His teaching career includes time with the University of Pennsylvania, the University of Wyoming, and the University of Massachusetts.

My Thoughts in Writing

1. On more than one occasion in his narrative, Wideman discusses or tries to define the purpose of stories. Find the places in the narrative where Wideman points out the usefulness of storytelling, where he seems to be trying to explain why we tell our stories in the first place. What purposes does he attribute to storytelling? How does he explain our need to turn our experiences into stories?

2. How is Wideman's story as much a story about his son as it is a story about himself and other members of his family? Is one story more important than another is? How do you know? How do all these individual stories contribute to Wideman's central theme?

3. Why does Wideman end the narrative as he does? What does time have to do with the human need, as Wideman sees it, to tell stories? How does storytelling connect Wideman to his people? How does it connect him—and us—to the past, present, and future?

———————— ✦ ————————

One day neither in the past nor in the future, and not at this moment, either, all the people gathered on a high ridge that overlooked the rolling plain of earth, its forests, deserts, rivers unscrolling below them like a painting on parchment. Then the people began speaking, one by one, telling the story of a life—everything seen, heard, and felt by each soul. As the voices dreamed, a vast, bluish mist enveloped the land and the seas below. Nothing was visible. It was as if the solid earth had evaporated. Now there was nothing but the voices and the stories and the mist; and the people were afraid to stop the storytelling and afraid not to stop, because no one knew where the earth had gone.

Finally, when only a few storytellers remained to take a turn, someone shouted: Stop! Enough, enough of this talk! Enough of us have spoken! We must find the earth again!

Suddenly, the mist cleared. Below the people, the earth had changed. It had grown into the shape of the stories they'd told— a shape as wondrous and new and real as the words they'd spoken. But it was also a world unfinished, because not all the stories had been told.

Some say that death and evil entered the world because some of the people had no chance to speak. Some say that the world would be worse than it is if all the stories had been told. Some say that there are no more stories to tell. Some believe that untold stories are the only ones of value and we are lost when they are lost. Some are certain that the storytelling never stops; and this is one more story, and the earth always lies under its blanket of mist being born.

I begin again because I don't want it to end. I mean all 5
these father stories that take us back, that bring us here, where you are, where I am, needing to make sense, to go on if we can and should.

Once, when you were five or six, all the keys to the camp vehicles disappeared. Keys for trucks, vans, rental cars, a school bus, a tractor, boats—the whole fleet necessary each summer to service the business of offering four hundred boys an eight-week escape in the Maine woods. In the innocence of the oasis that your grandfather had created—this gift of water, trees, a world apart—nobody bothered to lock things; keys were routinely left in the ignition for the next driver. Then, one day the keys were gone. For hours, everybody searched high and low. I thought of you as I climbed into the cab of the dump truck to check for a key that might have fallen to the floor or slipped into some crevice or corner of the raw, gasoline-reeking interior. You because countless times I'd hoisted you into the cab, tucked you in the driver's seat. Nothing you enjoyed more than turning a steering wheel, roaring and vrooming engine noise while you whipped the wheel back and forth, negotiating some endless, dramatic highway only you could see. You were fascinated by that imaginary road and the wheels that rolled you there. Even before you could talk, you'd flip your toy trucks and cars on their sides or upside down so you could spin the wheels, growl motor noise.

You never admitted taking the keys, and nobody pressed you very hard after they were found, in a heap in the sand under the boat dock. But, years later, Junie, the head caretaker, mentioned that he'd seen you making your usual early morning rounds from vehicle to vehicle the day the keys were missing, and confided to me a suspicion he had felt then but had kept to himself till you were gone and were unlikely to return for a long time. Turns out your grandfather had been suspicious, too. He didn't miss much that happened in the camp, either, and had observed what Junie had observed. I recall being rather annoyed when your grandfather suggested that I ask you if you might have noticed keys anywhere the day they disappeared. Annoyed and amazed, because you were hardly more than a baby. No reason for you to bother the keys. I'd instructed you never to touch them, and that was one of the conditions you'd promised to honor in return for the privilege of installing yourself behind steering wheels. I trusted you. Questioning my trust insulted us both. Besides, the missing keys implied a plot, a prank, sabotage, some scheme premeditated and methodically perpetrated by older campers or adults, and you were just a kid. You were my son. His grandson. So he gently hinted I might casually check with you, not because you were a suspect but because you had access and had been noticed at the scene, and so perhaps might be able to assist the searchers with a clue.

I don't remember your grandfather's ever mentioning the keys again until we'd lost you and all of us were searching once more for answers. And, since each of us had then begun to understand that answers were not around us, not in the air, and not exclusively in you, but inside us all, when your grandfather repeated ten years later his suspicions about the keys, it sounded almost like a confession, and we both understood that some searches never end.

A small army of adults, stymied, frustrated, turning the camp inside out. A couple of hours of mass confusion, pockets, drawers, memories rifled, conspiracy theories floated, paranoia blossoming, numb searches and re-searches. Minor panic when duplicate keys weren't stashed where they should be; righteous indignation and scapegoating; the buzz, the edge for weeks afterward whenever keys were mentioned, picked up, or set down in the camp office. The morning of the lost keys became one of those incidents, significant or not in themselves, that lend a name, a tone to a whole camp season: the summer of baby goats in the nature lodge, the hurricane summer, the summer a boy was lost for a night on Mt. Katahdin, the summer you-remember-who bit your grandfather's finger, the summer two counsellors from a boys' camp nearby were killed in a highspeed crash late at night, the summer the Israeli nurses swam topless, the summer you left and never returned.

If you'd ambled up on your short, chunky legs and handed   10 me the lost keys, it wouldn't have convinced me you'd taken them. Nor would a confession have convinced me. Nothing you might have said or done could have solved the mystery of the keys. No accident or coincidence would have implicated you. Without a reason, with no motive, no *why*, the idea of your removing the keys remained unthinkable.

You were blond then. Huge brown eyes. Hair on your head of many kinds, a storm, a multiculture of textures: kinky, dead straight, curly, frizzy, ringlets; hair thick in places, sparse in others. All your people, on both sides of the family, ecumenically represented in the golden crown atop your head.

You cried huge tears, too. Heartbreaking, slow, sliding tears that formed gradually in the corners of your dark eyes—gleaming, shapely tears before they collapsed and inched down your cheeks. Big tears, but you cried quietly, almost privately, even though the proof of your unhappiness was smearing your face. Then again, when you needed to, you could bellow and hoot—honking Coltrane explorations of anger, temper, outrage. Most of the time, however, you cried softly, your sobs pinched off by deep, heaving sighs, with a rare, high-pitched, keening wail escaping in spite of whatever was disciplining you to wrap your sorrow so close to yourself.

I'm remembering things in no order, with no plan. These father stories. Because that's all they are.

Your mother said that the story she wishes she could write, but knows is so painful she hesitates to tell it to herself, would be about her, of course, and you, yes, but also about her father, your grandfather: what he built, who he was, his long, special life, how many other lives he touched, the place he created out of nothing, in the woods, along the lake that I'm watching this morning, and that watches me as I write.

15   It is her father she has returned to all these summers in Maine. What he provided, no strings attached. His gift of water, trees, weather, a world apart, full of surprise, a world unchanging. Summers in Maine were the stable, rooted part of her.

One morning, as I sit on the dock staring at the lake, a man and a boy float past in a small boat. They have turned off the putt-putt outboard motor hanging over the stern and are drifting in closer to the rocky shore-line, casting their fishing lines where the water is blackish green from shadows of tall pines lining the lake. A wake spreads languidly behind the boat, one wing plowing the dark water, its twin unfurling like a bright flag dragged across the surface. No sound except bird-song, the hiss of a fishing line arcing away from the boat, then its plopping like a coin in the bottom of a well. The weather has changed overnight. Wind from the west this morning—a cooling, drying wind lifting the mist before dawn, turning the sky unwaveringly blue at this early hour. A wind shunting away last week's mugginess and humidity, though it barely ruffles the skin of the water in this inlet. Gray bands of different shades and textures stripe the lake's center, panels of a fan lazily unfolding, closing, opening. Later, the west wind will perk up and bring chill gusts, stir a chop into the water. Smooth and quiet now for the man and the boy hunkered down in their boat. They wear baseball caps, layers of shirts and jackets, the same bulky shape twice; one form is larger than the other, and each is a slightly different color, but otherwise the two are identical, down to the way their wrists snap, their lines arc up and away from the boat. The man's lure lands farther away than the boy's each time, in scale with the hunched figures drifting past in the boat.

I will see the boat again, about an hour later, when the water is louder, when ripples driven from the west are forming scalloped waves. The boy, alone then, whips the boat full throttle in tight, spray-sluicing circles, around and around, gouging deep furrows. The nose of the boat high in the air, he hunches over the screaming engine, gunning it in short, sprinting bursts, then in sharp turns, around and around, as if he were trying to escape a swarm of hornets.

The wind is forgetting it's July. I wish for extra insulation under my hooded sweatshirt and nylon windbreaker. Trees are a baffle for the wind and conjure its sound into colder, stronger, arctic messages shuttling through the upper atmosphere. In the same way, your mother's hair when it's long and loose, catching all the colors of light, falling down around her bare shoulders, carries within itself that wind rush of surf crashing far away, the muffled roar of a crowd in a vast, distant stadium.

You'd twist thick clumps of her chestnut hair in your fist, clutch it while she held you and you sucked the thumb of your other hand. For hours. For hours if she'd let you.

Maybe all things happen, including ourselves, long before   20 we see, hear, know they are happening. Memory, then, isn't so much archival as it is a seeking of vitality, harmony, an evocation of a truer, more nearly complete present tense. All of this, of course, relates to personality—the construction of a continuous narrative of self. Our stories. Father stories.

Do you remember your fear of leaves? Of course you do. The teasers in our family would never let you forget.

Once, in Laramie, Wyoming, after dinner, just as a full-moon night was falling and the wide, straight-arrow streets were as empty and still as Long Lake at dawn, I was riding you on my shoulders—a rare moment, the two of us together, away from your mother and brother—when, suddenly you cried out. The street we were on had a ceiling. Branches from trees planted in people's yards hung over fences lining the sidewalk, forming a canopy overhead. I panicked. Thought I'd knocked you against a low branch or you'd got your hair tangled—or, worse, been scratched in the eye or the face. Your fingers dug into my scalp. You didn't want to let go as I tried to unseat you from my shoulders, slide you down into the light from a street lamp to see what was the matter.

You'd given me a couple of good yanks, so I was both mad and scared when I finally pulled you down, cradling you in my arms to get a clear look at your face.

No tears. No visible damage. Yet you were wild-eyed, trembling uncontrollably. The leaves had been after you. Probably not touching you but, worse, a blanket of quivering, rustling, mottled dread suddenly hovering above you. Surrounding you, rendering you speechless. Terrorized beyond words or tears, you'd gripped my hair and kicked my chest. I'd thought you were roughing me up because you wanted to play. Grabbed your wrists and squeezed them tight to hold you as I galloped down the quiet Laramie street, doing my best imitation of the bucking bronco on Wyoming license plates. You were rendered even more helpless with your hands clamped in mine, struggling to free yourself while I thought we were having fun. Your father snorting and braying, jiggedy-jig, jiggedy-jig, suddenly in league with your worst enemy, and nowhere to run, nowhere to hide—he was rushing you to your doom. No wonder your fingers tried to rip my hair out when I released your wrists. Holding on, reining me in, pounding on my skull, fighting back the only way you knew how, short of pitching yourself down from a dizzying height, down, down to the pavement, itself strewn with shadowy leaves.

25 When I was a kid, I harbored a morbid fear of feathers. Feathers. Not a single feather or a few loose feathers, like the ones I'd stick in my naps to play Indian, but feathers in a bunch, attached to birds who could wriggle them, flutter them, transform them into loose flesh, rotting, molting, the unnatural sign of death-in-life and life-in-death, the zombie, mummy, decaying corpses of movies and my nightmares. Feathers a kind of squirmy skin hanging off the bone, all the more horrible because feathers seemed both dry and sticky with blood.

My feathers, your leaves. One afternoon at the Belmar on Homewood Avenue, in Pittsburgh, in one of those Bible-days epic movies, a man was tortured nearly to death, his bloody body flung off a fortress wall. He landed on a heap of corpses in a ditch. As the camera pans the mangled bodies, the sound of huge wings beating thumps through the Belmar's crackly speakers. After the Technicolor glare of carnage under a desert sun, the camera is blinded an instant by the black swoop of vultures. They land atop the corpses, feathers rippling, glinting as the birds begin their slow-motion, ponderously delicate lope toward the choicest morsels of meat—eyeballs, tongues, exposed guts—toward the not-quite-dead-yet man sprawled on a bed of other victims.

Then a closeup of the man's face. As he spots the vultures and screams, I scream. I know I did. Even though I couldn't hear myself, because everybody in the Belmar joined in one shrieking whoop of fear and disgust. And I never forgot the scene. Never. Never forgot, never forgave. Hated pigeons. They became my scapegoats, or scapebirds. I'd hurt them any chance I got. Trapped one in a box and tormented it. Fully intended to incinerate the crippled one who wound up on the stone steps in the hallway of my dorm freshman year until my roommate shamed me out of it when I asked to borrow his lighter and some fluid and he demanded to know for what.

Pigeons were brown and dirty. They shat everywhere. Spoiled things. Their cooing from the eaves of our roof on Finance Street could startle you awake. They sneaked around, hid in dark corners, carried disease, like rats. Far too many of the useless creatures. I focussed my fear and hate of feathers on them. Went out of my way to cause them difficulties.

Once, I was so angry at your mother's pain I thought I was angry at her. She was sharing out loud for the first time how torn apart she'd felt that summer you never came back. How she feared her father's gift had been blighted forever. Woods, lake, sky a mirror reflecting absence of father, absence of son, the presence of her grief.

I couldn't deal with the pain in her voice, so I made up another story. Presumed to tell her she was letting her pain exclude other ways of trying to make sense, with words, with stories, with the facts as given and the facts as felt, make sense of the enormity of what happens and doesn't happen, the glimmers of it we paste together trying to find peace. One different story would be the day she meets her father again in this place and what he might have to say to her and why he needed to see her and what he might remind her of and why it would need to

30

be here, on a path through the thick pine woods where light can surprise you, penetrating in smoky shafts where it has no business being, where it sparkles, then shifts instantly, gone faster than the noises of creatures in the underbrush you never see. I make up her father, as I'm making up mine. Her father appearing to her in a suit of lights because that, too, could transpire, could redeem, could set us straight in a world where you never know what's going to happen next and often what happens is bad, is crushing, but it's never the worst thing, never the best, it's only the last thing, and not even exactly that, except once, and even then death is not exactly the last thing that happens, because you never know what's going to happen next. For better or worse, cursed and blessed by this ignorance, we invent, fill it, are born with the gift, the need, the weight of filling it with our imaginings. That are somehow as real as we are. Our mothers and fathers and children. Our stories.

I hope this is not a hard day for you. I hope you can muster peace within yourself and deal with the memories, the horrors of the past eight years. It must strike you as strange—as strange as it strikes me—that eight years have passed already. I remember a few days after hearing you were missing and a boy was found dead in the room the two of you had been sharing, I remember walking down toward the lake to be alone, because I felt myself coming apart: the mask I'd been wearing, as much for myself as for the benefit of other people, was beginning to splinter. I could hear ice cracking, great rents and seams breaking my face into pieces, carrying away chunks of numb flesh. I found myself on my knees, praying to a tree. In the middle of some absurdly compelling ritual that I'd forgotten I carried the memory of. Yet there I was on my knees, digging my fingers into the loose soil, grabbing up handfuls, sinking my face into the clawed earth as if it might heal me. Speaking to the roots of a pine tree as if its shaft might carry my message up to the sky, send it on its way to wherever I thought my anguish should be addressed.

I was praying to join you. Offering myself in exchange for you. Take me. Take me. Free my son from the terrible things happening to him. Take me in his place. Let them happen to me. I was afraid you were dying or already dead or suffering unspeakable tortures at the hands of a demon kidnapper. The tears I'd held back were flowing finally, a flood that brought none of the relief I must have believed that hoarding them would earn me when I let go at last. Just wetness burning, clouding my eyes. I couldn't will the spirit out of my body into the high branches of that tree. What felt familiar, felt like prayers beside my bed as a child, or church people moaning in the amen corner, or my mother weeping and whispering *hold on, hold on* to herself as she rocks side to side and mourns, or some naked priest chanting and climbing toward the light on a bloody ladder inside his chest—these memories of what might have been visions of holiness could not change the simple facts. I was a man who had most likely lost his son, and hugging trees and burying his face in dirt and crying for help till breath slunk out of his body wouldn't change a thing.

A desperate, private moment, one of thousands I could force myself to dredge up if I believed it might serve some purpose. I share that one example with you to say that the eight years have not passed quickly. The years are countless moments, many as intense as this one I'm describing to you, moments I conceal from myself as I've hidden them from other people. Other moments, also countless, when terrible things had to be shared, spoken aloud, in phone calls with lawyers, depositions, interviews, conferences, in the endless conversations with your mother. Literally endless, because often the other business of our lives would seem merely a digression from the dialogue with you, about you. A love story finally, love of you, your brother and sister, since no word except love makes sense of the ever-present narrative our days unfold.

Time can drag like a long string, studded and barbed, through a fresh wound, so it hasn't gone quickly. The moment-to-moment, day-by-day struggles imprint my flesh. But the eight years are also a miracle, a blink of the eye through which I watch myself wending my way from there to here. In this vast house of our fathers and mothers.

Your mother didn't need my words or images to work out her grief. She needed time. Took the time she needed to slowly, gradually, painstakingly unravel feelings knotted in what seemed for a while a hopeless tangle. No choice, really. She's who she is. Can give nothing less than her whole heart to you, to this place, inseparable from all our lives, that her father, your grandfather, provided.

For a while, I guess it must have felt impossible. And still can, I know. She may have doubted her strength, her capacity to give enough, give everything, because everything seemed to be tearing her apart, breaking her down. She needed time. Not healing time, exactly, since certain wounds never heal, but time to change and more time to learn to believe, to understand she could go on, was going on, for better or worse. She could be someone she'd never dreamed she could be. Her heart strong, whole, even as it cracks and each bit demands everything.

The fullness of time. The fullness of time. That phrase has haunted me since I first heard it or read it, though I don't know when or how the words entered my awareness, because they seem to have always been there, like certain melodies, for instance, or visual harmonies of line in your mother's body that I wondered how I'd ever lived without the first time I encountered them, although another recognition clicked in almost simultaneously, reminding me that I'd been waiting for those particular notes, those lines, a very long time. They'd been forming me before I formed my first impressions of them.

The fullness of time. Neither forward nor backward. A space capacious enough to contain your coming into and going out of the world, your consciousness of these events, the wrap of oblivion bedding them. A life, the passage of a life: the truest understanding, measure, experience of time's fullness. So many lives, and each different, each unknowable, no matter how similar to yours, your flesh and not your flesh, lives passing, like yours, into the fullness of time, where each of these lives and all of them together make no larger ripple than yours, all and each abiding in the unruffled innocence of the fullness that is time. All the things that mattered so much to you or them sinking into a dreadful, unfeatured equality that is also rest and peace, time gone: but more, always more, the hands writing, the hands snatching, hands becoming bones, then dust, then whatever comes next, what time takes and fashions of you after the possibilities, permutations, and combinations—the fullness in you— are exhausted, played out for the particular shape the fullness has assumed for a time in you, for you. You are never it but what it could be, then is not: you not lost but ventured, gained, stretched, more, until the dust is particles and the particles play unhindered, unbound, returned to the fullness of time.

I know my father's name, Edgar, and some of his fathers' names, Hannibal, Tatum, Jordan, but I can't go back any further than a certain point, except that I also know the name of a place, Greenwood, South Carolina, and an even smaller community, Promised Land, nearly abutting Greenwood, where my grandfather, who, of course, is your great-grandfather, was born, and where many of his brothers are buried, under sturdy tombstones bearing his name, our name, "Wideman," carved in stone in the place where the origins of the family name begin to dissolve into the loam of plantations owned by white men, where my grandfathers' identities dissolve, where they were boys, then men, and the men they were fade into a set of facts, sparse, ambiguous, impersonal, their intimate lives unretrievable, where what is known about a country, a region, a country and its practice of human bondage, its tradition of obscuring, stealing, or distorting black people's lives, begins to crowd out the possibility of seeing my ancestors as human beings. The powers and principalities that originally restricted our access to the life that free people naturally enjoy still rise like a shadow, a wall between my grandfathers and me, my father and me, between the two of us, father and son, son and father.

So we must speak these stories to one another.   40
Love.

Remembering Lobo
Pat Mora

Born in El Paso, Texas, in 1942, Pat Mora received a bachelor's degree in 1963 from Texas Western College and a master's degree from the University of Texas at El Paso in 1967. Mora has written three collections of poetry and a number of books for children. Her personal commentaries, like the following selection, reflect her interest in how individuals maintain and celebrate cultural identity.

My Thoughts in Writing

1. Some of our family stories focus on nicknames and naming practices. Mora's story is one of these. How does Mora justify giving the nickname "Lobo" (meaning "Wolf" in Spanish) to her "generous and loving aunt"? What aspects of her aunt's behavior make Lobo an apt nickname? What other details about Lobo can you gather from Mora's narrative? Do these details help you understand the nickname or other aspects of Lobo's personality?

2. Why do you think Mora is writing about Lobo? Besides her nickname, what about Lobo makes her worthy of a story? Why do you think Mora switches from telling her story about Lobo to Lobo telling her own story in the end? What is the effect of this switch?

3. What is the central theme of Mora's piece? Is it stated in the text or implied? If it is not stated in the text, put it in your own words and explain how you came to your answer.

─────────────── ✦ ───────────────

We called her *Lobo*. The word means "wolf" in Spanish, an odd name for a generous and loving aunt. Like all names it became synonymous with her, and to this day returns me to my childself. Although the name seemed perfectly natural to us and to our friends, it did cause frowns from strangers throughout the years. I particularly remember one hot afternoon when on a crowded streetcar between the border cities of El Paso and Juarez, I momentarily lost sight of her. "Lobo! Lobo!" I cried in panic. Annoyed faces peered at me, disappointed at such disrespect to a white-haired woman.

Actually the fault was hers. She lived with us for years, and when she arrived home from work in the evening, she'd knock on our front door and ask, "¿ *Dónde están mis lobitos?*" "Where are my little wolves?"

Gradually she became our *lobo,* a spinster aunt who gathered the four of us around her, tying us to her for life by giving us all she had. Sometimes to tease her we would call her by her real name. "¿ *Dónde está Ignacia?*" we would ask. Lobo would laugh and say, "She is a ghost."

To all of us in nuclear families today, the notion of an extended family under one roof seems archaic, complicated. We treasure our private space. I will always marvel at the generosity of my parents, who opened their door to both my grandmother and Lobo. No doubt I am drawn to the elderly because I grew up with two entirely different white-haired women who worried about me, tucked me in at night, made me tomato soup or hot *hierbabuena* (mint tea) when I was ill.

Lobo grew up in Mexico, the daughter of a circuit judge,   5 my grandfather. She was a wonderful storyteller and over and over told us about the night her father, a widower, brought his grown daughters on a flat-bed truck across the Rio Grande at the time of the Mexican Revolution. All their possessions were left in Mexico. Lobo had not been wealthy, but she had probably never expected to have to find a job and learn English.

When she lived with us, she worked in the linens section of a local department store. Her area was called "piece goods and bedding." Lobo never sewed, but she would talk about materials she sold, using words I never completely understood, such as *pique* and *broadcloth*. Sometimes I still whisper such words just to remind myself of her. I'll always savor the way she would order "sweet milk" at restaurants. The precision of a speaker new to the language.

Lobo saved her money to take us out to dinner and a movie, to take us to Los Angeles in the summer, to buy us shiny black shoes for Christmas. Though she never married and never bore children, Lobo taught me much about one of our greatest challenges as human beings: loving well. I don't think she ever discussed the subject with me, but through the years she lived her love, and I was privileged to watch.

She died at ninety-four. She was no sweet, docile Mexican woman dying with perfect resignation. Some of her last words before drifting into semiconsciousness were loud words of annoyance at the incompetence of nurses and doctors.

"*No sirven.*" "They're worthless," she'd say to me in Spanish.
10   "They don't know what they're doing. My throat is hurting and they're taking X rays. Tell them to take care of my throat first."

I was busy striving for my cherished middle-class politeness. "Shh, shh," I'd say. "They're doing the best they can."

"Well, it's not good enough," she'd say, sitting up in anger.

Lobo was a woman of fierce feelings, of strong opinions. She was a woman who literally whistled while she worked. The best way to cheer her when she'd visit my young children was to ask for her help. Ask her to make a bed, fold laundry, set the table or dry dishes, and the whistling would begin as she moved about her task. Like all of us, she loved being needed. Understandable, then, that she muttered in annoyance when her body began to fail her. She was a woman who found self-definition and joy in visibly showing her family her love for us by bringing us hot *té de canela* (cinnamon tea) in the middle of the night to ease a cough, by bringing us comics and candy whenever she returned home. A life of giving.

One of my last memories of her is a visit I made to her on November 2, *El Día de los Muertos,* or All Souls' Day. She was sitting in her rocking chair, smiling wistfully. The source of the smile may seem a bit bizarre to a U.S. audience. She was fondly remembering past visits to the local cemetery on this religious feast day.

15   "What a silly old woman I have become," she said. "Here I sit in my rocking chair all day on All Souls' Day, sitting when I should be out there. At the cemetery. Taking good care of *mis muertos,* my dead ones.

"What a time I used to have. I'd wake while it was still dark outside. I'd hear the first morning birds, and my fingers would almost itch to begin. By six I'd be having a hot bath, dressing carefully in black, wanting *mis muertos* to be proud of me, proud to have me looking respectable and proud to have their graves taken care of. I'd have my black coffee and plenty of toast. You know the way I like it. Well browned and well buttered. I wanted to be ready to work hard.

"The bus ride to the other side of town was a long one, but I'd say a rosary and plan my day. I'd hope that my perfume wasn't too strong and yet would remind others that I was a lady.

"The air at the cemetery gates was full of chrysanthemums: that strong, sharp, fall smell. I'd buy tin cans full of the gold and wine flowers. How I liked seeing aunts and uncles who were also there to care for the graves of their loved ones. We'd hug. Happy together.

"Then it was time to begin. The smell of chrysanthemums was like a whiff of pure energy. I'd pull the heavy hose and wash the gravestones over and over, listening to the water pelting away the desert sand. I always brought newspaper. I'd kneel on the few patches of grass, and I'd scrub and scrub, shining the gray stones, leaning back on my knees to rest for a bit and then scrubbing again. Finally a relative from nearby would say, '*Ya, ya, Nacha,*' and laugh. Enough. I'd stop, blink my eyes to return from my trance. Slightly dazed, I'd stand slowly, place a can of chrysanthemums before each grave.

"Sometimes I would just stand there in the desert sun and listen. I'd hear the quiet crying of people visiting new graves; I'd hear families exchanging gossip while they worked.   20

"One time I heard my aunt scolding her dead husband. She'd sweep his gravestone and say, '*¿ Porqué?* Why did you do this, you thoughtless man? Why did you go and leave me like this? You know I don't like to be alone. Why did you stop living?' Such a sight to see my aunt with her proper black hat and her fine dress and her carefully polished shoes muttering away for all to hear.

"To stifle my laughter, I had to cover my mouth with my hands."

Joy of Funerals

ALIX STRAUSS

Freelance writer and actress Alix Strauss (born in 1968) lives in New York City. Formerly Nurse Sharon on the soap opera *As the World Turns,* Strauss received a bachelor's degree in liberal arts and a degree in English education from New York University.

My Thoughts in Writing

1. What is the mood of Strauss's piece? How does it relate to the selection's theme? What message is Strauss trying to convey and how do families and family stories fit into that central message?
2. Strauss writes that "paying respect at a relative's home is like finding a secret stash of candy." When she goes to the homes of relatives, what does she find that is like a secret stash of candy?
3. Strauss is drawn to the "relative who can tell a story, embellish a tale or two." How are the stories like puzzle pieces for her? Why are they so important? What does she learn or gain from them?

In the winter, everyone is matted down in thick wool coats, standing in a huddled mass of sniffles and tears. In the summer, the air rings full of sorrow as mourners sigh, their cotton jackets and black dresses blowing in the breeze. To me, it doesn't matter in what season a funeral takes place. I enjoy them just the same.

While my relatives try to collect themselves—some bursting into moments of hysterics—I feel an excitement, a back-to-school restlessness that overrides my grief. My unnatural joy for family gatherings stems from the lack thereof. Because I come from such a small clan, funerals are my only real chance to make contact with relatives I haven't seen in years.

When I was a child, everyone else's family tree seemed like a strong, robust oak; mine was more like a weeping willow, broken and hanging low. For me, there were no holiday dinners spent bonding over burned turkey and overcooked stuffing, no long-distance, late-night phone calls, no group vacations, no sharing of conquered milestones with family members. It is the "where do I belong?" and "where do I come from?" that is missing from my life. The longing for a connection to someone or something is a feeling I have never been able to let go of.

It's because I am an only child. Actually, I am the only only child. For as many generations as I can retrace, everyone in my family has had several children—except, of course, my parents, who decided to have just me. Although each of my parents has a sibling, neither is especially close to them.

Paying final respects at a relative's home is like finding a secret stash of candy. I can't help but inspect each room, searching through cabinets and dresser drawers, looking through scrapbooks and photo albums filled with old Kodak memories: my grandmother and her sisters sunning at the Plaza Beach Club, my mother's 12th birthday party, my father's Army troop. Snap, a moment is captured. Tangible evidence of time. Proof of existence. Validation. ⁵

I snoop in the hopes of finding answers about who they are; I search for something that will connect me to them. I often find myself staring at my relatives—these strangers, this handful of souls, to help define me. I rely on them to tell stories about my grandparents and other family members from days of long ago—the clock I can't turn back.

I am drawn to the relative who can tell a story, embellish a tale or two about my mother when she was 6 or 7 or call my father by an old nickname he has outgrown, embarrassing him with information privy only to an insider. With these family members there is a level of understanding and forgiveness that can't be re-created with others entering my life now. They are bookmarks in my past as we reminisce about the only thing we have in common.

Conversations pick up exactly where they left off years ago. And as we share stories of the recently deceased, a small puzzle piece slips quietly into place. It is this inner imageless object I have been trying to complete for years. An empty space waiting to be filled with answers and belonging. Like it or not, there are similarities we share—left-handedness, hair and eye color, mannerisms—qualities from an exclusive gene pool. I know I have a connection that can't be erased, ignored or changed. It is through understanding them that I will be better able to understand myself.

I have discussed my appetite for funerals with other only children, all of whom come from small families, and they, too, share my unnatural excitement for these ancestral events. As an only child, no matter how hard I try, I still feel an emptiness during the major holidays, a jealousy when I see sisters walking down the street, arms locked, or families laughing together in sync. And there is a loneliness and sense of loss that follows me wherever I go, as if I have forgotten something.

10   So I wait. I wait for events that will bring my family together. I wait for parties, weddings and birth announcements. But none come. There was a time, however, when my parents were included in all fun functions. But as with most families, gaps, misunderstandings, grudges and age differences have helped break apart and split my family tree. So I wait instead for funerals. Everyone is included; everyone deserves a chance to say goodbye.

Through sorrow and through consoling, I am needed. I am part of something whole. I have made a difference in their lives, even if just for a short while.

When the day is over and people have changed out of black into more comfortable, less formal clothing, I may be forgotten. But the day, the meaningful time we have spent bonding as a family, will always be a part of my life.

Sample Student Essay

My Special Place

KRISTEN JACOMINO

My father was taken from my life just two weeks after my birth. Except he wasn't really taken; he left. He left my mom and me in New Jersey to start a new life with his new wife in Fort Collins, Colorado. When I turned the legal adult age of eighteen, I decided it was time to meet my seemingly nonexistent father. This was sure to be an awkward experience, but an experience I felt had to happen. What I came to realize was that sometimes events that we are unsure of end up being the most important ones of all, the ones with the power to change our lives.

In the weeks prior to my departure to meet my dad in Colorado, the nerves set in. It felt like hundreds of controlling butterflies had taken up residency in my stomach. During that time, food was not welcome in my belly, but it was surely encouraged to exit. I also seemed to have acquired another nuisance: tension headaches. This type of headache starts in the shoulders and slowly creeps its way up to the base of the skull. It felt like I was carrying a domineering and unstable elephant on my neck. Preparing to leave for Colorado was like conditioning for a race. I would do warms-ups and practice runs—deciding on outfits to wear and different strategies to put in action should I come across a worrisome situation—like not recognizing my father at the airport or simply suddenly changing my mind halfway there. Yet, like a race, I knew once my trip started that everything would be complete chaos until I found my balance. I was hoping I could do this without tripping.

I arrived in Colorado on a crisp, clear morning in April. I remember walking down the plane's long, unstable corridor, wondering if my dad would know who I was or what I looked like. "What do I say to him?" I kept thinking. "What will he say to me?" Then I saw him. He seemed larger-than-life standing there in front of me. He stood a broad six foot four inches, and he was wearing a brightly colored Southwestern-influenced shirt and faded blue jeans. On his feet were the cleanest, brownest cowboy boots I had ever seen. Atop his unfamiliar head proudly sat a deep chestnut cowboy hat. It was all I could do not to ask, "John Wayne?" But before I had a chance to say anything, he embraced me, holding me so tightly to him I felt as though he were afraid I would slip away. When he finally let me go, we began walking to the baggage claim. During our walk, we chatted uncomfortably. Finally, it was time to leave the stuffy airport. I was not prepared for what was to hit me outside those thick airport doors.

When we stepped outside, I took my first breath of Colorado air. My nose filled with the aromas of melting ice; freshly mowed grass; and sweet, sweet lilac. My lungs expanded with a burst of energy; my spirits felt rejuvenated. Heading toward my dad's dusty white Suburban, I saw them: the Colorado Rocky Mountains. They took me off guard, those magnificent mounds escaping from the dull ground, their peaks extending upward in majestic beauty. Tranquil grays and blues drew me in, and pure, pure whiteness paralyzed my eyes; I could not look away. Enormous clouds engulfed the jagged peaks, forbidding me to see any more. On the long drive to my father's house, I unintentionally ignored his attempts at conversation. Something else had my attention, something greater than anything I had ever known.

My time spent with my father and his family paled in comparison to the time I spent by myself in Colorado. I would sit for hours just breathing, not thinking about anything, but thinking about everything. The air was so chaste and untainted, every breath like a hit of pure oxygen. I could stand in the middle of a field, look in one direction, and see straight into Kansas. There were no trees or strip malls, just space, space into which I could disappear had I wanted to. If I turned directly around, I would be staring into the face of those enormous, somewhat presumptuous mountains. I felt sometimes as though they were drawing me to them, upward, freely. My headaches disappeared and that two-ton elephant walked right off my shoulders and away. I was free; everything was much clearer now. I realized how much I had been missing, how much more there was of the world for me to see. The awkwardness between my father and me dissipated as I came to this clarity of mind and spirit. We had one precious thing in common—Colorado—and that was enough.

I knew leaving my place of enlightenment would be the most difficult thing I would have to do. Still, after ten of the most inspirational days in my life, I went home. Flying into Philadelphia, I looked down into the cesspool of that "magnificent city" and thought about how tainted and accelerated my life (and all our lives) had become. Essentially, I thought, if we could just stop and take a deep breath, exhale all of our troubles, our lives would be so much sweeter.

After arriving home, I realized I had left something behind in Colorado. I had left my internal baggage, my heavy, burdensome suitcase. I don't think I'll miss it. Since my experience in Colorado, I have pulled my life together, I have become a new person, a new and improved me. For example, I lost seventy-two pounds and my insecurity. I have become much healthier and more self-confident. I have also enrolled full-time in college with the assurance that I will be something. The biggest perk of my trip is that I am now happy, happier than I have ever been. If I had never had that awkward experience with my father, I would not be the person I am today, a person who knows that if I don't take risks in life, I'll never be complete. I don't want to risk that.

My Thoughts in Writing

1. Jacomino uses vivid sensory detail to illustrate the stress she experienced prior to meeting her father. What senses does she evoke and which sensory details are most effective? Where else in the essay does she include sensory details to make you feel as though you are there with her, experiencing things as she does?
2. To lighten up this serious story, Jacomino tries her hand at humor on numerous occasions. Find the places where she adds humor to her story and determine whether her attempts at humor work. Explain your answer using the text to make your point.
3. Why might Jacomino feel this story is worth sharing with others? What is her central theme and how relevant is it to a general audience?

The Readings Come Together

1. How are the selections by Wideman, Mora, and Strauss similar in terms of their messages about the role of storytelling in all our lives?
2. How is the atmosphere or mood of Wideman's selection similar to the atmosphere or mood of Strauss's? Of Jacomino's? How does mood affect

each piece? How does mood help each author convey his or her message about families, family stories, storytellers, or storytelling?

3. In their works, both Wideman and Mora do something unique with narration. Wideman uses third person, addressing his work to his lost son, and Mora allows her aunt to tell her own story at the end of the work. Regarding story and storytelling, what can be learned from the effectiveness of these two narrative strategies? How do they speak to the uniqueness of all individual stories?

4. Which selections contain a story within a story? How are these selections similar? How do they differ? What is the purpose of this technique? What aspects of storytelling does this technique reflect?

5. Compare and contrast the role of setting in the works by Strauss and Jacomino. What is the relationship between setting and theme in both selections? How does each writer articulate that relationship?

There's Something More out There

Part I

At-Home Activity

Options

- Interview a couple in your family/community (perhaps your parents) about how they met, their first dating experiences, and so on. Then, in your journal, record the story of their courtship.
- After interviewing family/community members or doing research on the Internet or in the library, record in your journal how your family/community came to live where they do—city or town and state.
- In your journal, record stories your family/community tells about pets. Such stories are often referred to as pet legends.
- Brainstorm with extended family/community members for family/community stories you have never been told. Record one or more in your journal.
- Record a story a family/community member tells when he or she wants to tease or embarrass you.
- Record a humorous story you tell about yourself just to make others laugh or to convey an impression about yourself.

Part II

Classroom Storytelling Session

The stories we tell, the stories told about us, and tales about the good taletellers in our lives. Create a classroom storytelling circle and share some of the stories collected during the above exercise.

Part III

Journal Entry

Option 1. Write a story that someone in your family or community tells about another member in order to preserve history.

Option 2. Write a story that someone in your family or community tells you in order to preserve a family tradition.

Option 3. Write a story about someone in your family or community who knows how to tell a good story.

Part IV

Writing Assignment

Using one of the reading selections as a way of approaching your subject, create an essay based on one of your journal entries. Make sure your essay makes clear the relationship you find between your work and the reading selection you use to approach your own study. Ask yourself: Why is this story told? What is the relevance of this story? What lesson/tradition/behavior is it meant to convey?

Oral Presentation Assignment (Optional)

Using one of the reading selections as a way of approaching your subject, prepare a presentation based on one of your journal entries. In preparing your oral narrative presentation, focus on clarifying what you believe the writer's purpose is in writing and the relationship you see between the writer's story and the one you are prepared to share with your class. As you practice telling your story, pay special attention to developing sensory details to create immediacy. Consider how you might engage your audience in the oral narrative you are sharing. What are your reasons for sharing this narrative? What would you like it to convey? What lessons can be learned from the experience encapsulated in your oral narrative? Can you convey the lesson to your audience without coming right out and saying it?

Folklore and the Search for Self

THE FOLKLORE FOCUS

Folk Traditions, Communal Values, and Personal Identity

About her hometown a friend once said to me: "I love the place; it's so full of tradition." When I asked her to elaborate, she rattled off—in chronological order—an impressive list of traditional events that the members of her community engaged in each year. There was the New Year's parade down Main Street, the Valentine's Ball at the community center, the March Mayhem Dinner and Dance at the fire hall, the Easter Egg Hunt at the park, the May Days Yard Sale Weekend, the Celebrate Summer Festival, the Labor Day Community Picnic, and the list goes on. Among these traditions, there are those common to other communities, some that have to do with religion, and others that are strictly of the community's own making. Whichever the type, each of these traditions offers something unique to the members of this community. For instance, the Yard Sale Weekend gives people a chance to empty out their houses and refill them again with "new" things; the March Mayhem Dinner and Dance presents a much-needed fun occasion during that cloudy time between bitter winter and sweet spring; and the Celebrate Summer Festival provides community members an opportunity to welcome the vacation season. In many ways, these traditions shape this community, giving it a distinct identity. And while each tradition serves its own function, together they fulfill a common purpose: to make the community just that, a community.

Traditions such as those mentioned may not interest all members of a community, but chances are, in most communities, enough members do take part to make such traditions a given when officials go about planning the yearly community calendar. Nevertheless, should a tradition lose its appeal or should an occasion arise that calls for a new one, no doubt the community would plan accordingly. This is the way it works in most groups. That is, most of us have a set of traditions in which we engage and, for the most part, to which we look forward. These traditions play a large part in our idea of who we are and where we belong. Moreover, whether we recognize it or not, it is by these traditions that we structure our lives—measure our days and show evidence of what matters most to us.

A good many people plan their lives according to the traditions in which they engage. The date books in their heads, if not their actual pocket calendars, are full of notations and reminders regarding birthdays, holidays, family gatherings, monthly dinners, anniversaries, and the like. When one tradition comes and goes, the countdown begins for the next one. Recurring yearly traditions such as birthdays and anniversaries and even situational traditions such as funerals and baby showers mark the passing of days, months, and years. They show evidence of lives in motion, moving constantly forward. Without these traditions to which these people look forward and for which they plan, a certain amount of structure would be missing from their lives. Even more significant, however, would be the loss of a kind of "meaning to life" many find by engaging in these traditions. In addition, whether it is a recurring tradition or a situational tradition, these folkloric engagements seem to remind us of what matters most and help us illustrate just that—what matters most to us. They become our way of (re)affirming and demonstrating what we value.

This chapter encourages you to study the various traditions we engage in as families and/or communities and to study the purpose(s) of these traditions. The readings selected for this chapter and the questions that follow them will help you do this. While each selection highlights the significance of one or many traditions, together they illustrate both the variety of traditions out there and what those traditions have in common. The questions that follow each selection require you to further analyze the readings, to examine what is being said about tradition's role in the lives of individuals and/or communities. Pay close attention to the way the writers use vivid sensory detail and a variety of narrative techniques to bring their experiences to life and to help you understand the meaning of the traditions described. Your careful study of these selections and the various traditions they present will prepare you for writing about the many traditions that shape your life. To begin thinking about these traditions, ask yourself: What are the traditions we (your family and/or community) engage in each year? What does each tradition entail? Why do we continue these traditions? What purposes do they serve? These questions will help you determine the various forms of folklore you engage in and prepare you to convey the meaning of that folklore in writing.

All the World's a Festival

JOE VERGARA

In his memoir *Love and Pasta*, from which the following excerpt is taken, Joe Vergara chronicles his life as the child of Italian immigrants. The richness of Vergara's heritage remains a high point in his memory of his very Italian cultured life.

My Thoughts in Writing

1. Vergara's father told him that in southern Italy, his homeland, "the confetti from one festa had hardly been swept up when preparations began for the next." What reasons are given for so many festivals? If there wasn't a festival planned, how did people make up for the lack of one?

2. Although Vergara mentions many festivals, the process of only one is described in detail. Why does Vergara remember this festival so well? What made the Madonna Dolorata festival particularly attractive to Joe and his brothers?
3. How does Vergara feel about the festivals of his homeland? How do you know? According to Vergara, what was the purpose of all the traditional celebrations of his homeland? How does he explain this purpose to his sons?

——————— ✦ ———————

For Pop loved festivals, those carefree breaks in the dull routine of living. In America, Pop complained, festivals were much too rare and too tame for his taste.

"What people do for good a time?" he grumbled. "Maybe they go see movie-a pitch', or maybe base-a ball. All-a time watch. Nobody dance-a, nobody laugh-a, nobody sing-a. Just-a watch." From Pop's tone, it was clear he considered watching an invention of the devil.

But in southern Italy it was different. As Pop told it, the confetti from one festa had hardly been swept up when preparations began for the next. And there was never a shortage of pretexts. As a starter, there were the saints, one for every day. Then, of course, the Blessed Virgin and the Holy Infant. Every town had its own patron saint and its quota of distinguished citizens and religious celebrities who rated festivals. If reasons for a festa ran thin, the people could celebrate the harvest, the squeezing of the grapes, the pressing of the olives. Any lulls were filled by parties celebrating births, weddings, christenings, funerals. So if you could move from place to place fast enough, life could be one merry round of festivals.

Pop's voice as he described these fun-filled festivals dripped with nostalgia. We were enthralled by his description of the Madonna Dolorata festival, held in his home town. Right after Mass, a dozen carefully chosen young men, dressed in medieval costume, lifted a huge statue of the Madonna onto their shoulders and carried it through the brightly decorated streets up the mountain and back, accompanied by three bands and the entire population of the town. Pop and the other little boys would run from one end of the procession to the other, now cheering the men struggling up the mountain with their heavy burden, now encouraging the bands to play louder and faster. During their run, they gaily tripped up any little girls in their way, and they stopped only to stock up on spumoni and lemon ices. Now and then, one of the townspeople would break through the crowd and pin some paper money on the ribbons bedecking the statue. When the procession returned to the church, the merry-making began. While the three bands alternated, the populace let itself go in a great emotional explosion—dancing, singing, joking, drinking, eating.

We kids found Pop's picture of a world of continuous merriment fascinating. When he finished telling us about the Madonna Dolorata festival, I asked him why he had ever consented to leave such a happy land. At my question, he became oddly serious.   5

"I tell-a you only nice-a part," he said, with a sad little smile. "How I can explain? It's-a like funny bird who all-a time sing. He don' sing-a because he's happy. He sing-a because he's afraid."

At the time, this made no sense to me. Now I understand. Life in poverty-filled southern Italy was hard, the rewards meager. But, even worse, the future held little promise—just more of the same. Talent, ability, ambition couldn't grow on the poor soil. To make everyday life bearable, the resourceful people organized festivals.

Fiesta

Octavio Paz

Octavio Paz (1914–1998) was born in Mexico City and served as a Mexican diplomat in France and Japan and as ambassador to India. His volumes of poetry and his work as an essayist earned him the Nobel Prize for Literature in 1990. Like so much of his work, the following essay reflects Paz's concern for accurate portrays of Latin American cultures.

My Thoughts in Writing

1. According to Paz, why does the "solitary Mexican" love fiestas? What is so special about these festivals? Why, in Paz's opinion, are such festivals rare in wealthy countries?
2. In his essay, Paz describes more than one type of festival. List the types of festivals he describes. How do they differ? How are they similar?
3. How do the fiestas serve individuals? What common social purpose is served by the festivals Paz describes? What do they give Mexicans a chance to do? What does Paz mean when he writes that these fiestas are a "revolution," a "plunge into chaos" (par. 10 and 11). Based on your own experience, is this description correct? Explain your answer.

———————— ✦ ————————

The solitary Mexican loves fiestas and public gatherings. Any occasion for getting together will serve, any pretext to stop the flow of time and commemorate men and events with festivals and ceremonies. We are a ritual people, and this characteristic enriches both our imaginations and our sensibilities, which are equally sharp and alert. The art of the fiesta has been debased almost everywhere else, but not in Mexico. There are few places in the world where it is possible to take part in a spectacle like our great religious fiestas with their violent primary colors, their bizarre costumes and dances, their fireworks and ceremonies and their inexhaustible welter of surprises: the fruit, candy, toys and other objects sold on these days in the plazas and open-air markets.

Our calendar is crowded with fiestas. There are certain days when the whole country, from the most remote villages to the largest cities, prays, shouts, feasts, gets drunk and kills, in honor of the Virgin of Guadalupe or Benito Juaréz. Each year on the fifteenth of September, at eleven o'clock at night, we celebrate the fiesta of the *Grito* in all the plazas of the Republic, and the excited crowds actually shout for a whole hour . . . the better, perhaps, to remain silent for the rest of the year. During the days before and after the twelfth of December, time comes to a full stop, and instead of pushing us toward a deceptive tomorrow that is always beyond our reach, offers us a complete and perfect today of dancing and revelry, of communion with the most ancient and secret Mexico. Time is no longer succession, and becomes what it originally was and is: the present, in which past and future are reconciled.

But the fiestas which the Church and State provide for the country as a whole are not enough. The life of every city and village is ruled by a patron saint whose blessing is celebrated with devout regularity. Neighborhoods and trades also have their annual fiestas, their ceremonies and fairs. And each one of us—atheist, Catholic, or merely indifferent—has his own saint's day, which he observes every year. It is impossible to calculate how many fiestas we have and how much time and money we spend on them. I remember asking the mayor of a village near Mitla, several years ago, "What is the income of the village government?" "About 3,000 pesos a year. We are very poor. But the Governor and the Federal Government always help us to meet our expenses." "And how are the 3,000 pesos spent?" "Mostly on fiestas, señor. We are a small village, but we have two patron saints."

This reply is not surprising. Our poverty can be measured by the frequency and luxuriousness of our holidays. Wealthy countries have very few: there is neither the time nor the desire for them, and they are not necessary. The people have other things to do, and when they amuse themselves they do so in small groups. The modern masses are agglomerations of solitary individuals. On great occasions in Paris or New York, when the populace gathers in the squares or stadiums, the absence of people, in the sense of *a* people, is remarkable: there are couples and small groups, but they never form a living community in which the individual is at once dissolved and redeemed. But how could a poor Mexican live without the two or three annual fiestas that make up for his poverty and misery? Fiestas are our only luxury. They replace, and are perhaps better than, the theater and vacations, Anglo-Saxon weekends and cocktail parties, the bourgeois reception, the Mediterranean café.

In all of these ceremonies—national or local, trade or 5
family—the Mexican opens out. They all give him a chance to reveal himself and to converse with God, country, friends or relations. During these days the silent Mexican whistles,

shouts, sings, shoots off fireworks, discharges his pistol into the air. He discharges his soul. And his shout, like the rockets we love so much, ascends to the heavens, explodes into green, red, blue, and white lights, and falls dizzily to earth with a trail of golden sparks. This is the night when friends who have not exchanged more than the prescribed courtesies for months get drunk together, trade confidences, weep over the same troubles, discover that they are brothers, and sometimes, to prove it, kill each other. The night is full of songs and loud cries. The lover wakes up his sweetheart with an orchestra. There are jokes and conversations from balcony to balcony, sidewalk to sidewalk. Nobody talks quietly. Hats fly in the air. Laughter and curses ring like silver pesos. Guitars are brought out. Now and then, it is true, the happiness ends badly, in quarrels, insults, pistol shots, stabbings. But these too are part of the fiesta, for the Mexican does not seek amusement: he seeks to escape from himself, to leap over the wall of solitude that confines him during the rest of the year. All are possessed by violence and frenzy. Their souls explode like the colors and voices and emotions. Do they forget themselves and show their true faces? Nobody knows. The important thing is to go out, open a way, get drunk on noise, people, colors. Mexico is celebrating a fiesta. And this fiesta, shot through with lightning and delirium, is the brilliant reverse to our silence and apathy, our reticence and gloom.

According to the interpretation of French sociologists, the fiesta is an excess, an expense. By means of this squandering the community protects itself against the envy of the gods or of men. Sacrifices and offerings placate or buy off the gods and the patron saints. Wasting money and expending energy affirms the community's wealth in both. This luxury is a proof of health, a show of abundance and power. Or a magic trap. For squandering is an effort to attract abundance by contagion. Money calls to money. When life is thrown away it increases; the orgy, which is sexual expenditure, is also a ceremony of regeneration; waste gives strength. New Year celebrations, in every culture, signify something beyond the mere observance of a date on the calendar. The day is a pause: time is stopped, is actually annihilated. The rites that celebrate its death are intended to provoke its rebirth, because they mark not only the end of an old year but also the beginning of a new. Everything attracts its opposite. The fiesta's function, then, is more utilitarian than we think: waste attracts or promotes wealth, and is an investment like any other, except that the returns on it cannot be measured or counted. What is sought is potency, life, health. In this sense the fiesta, like the gift and the offering, is one of the most ancient of economic forms.

This interpretation has always seemed to me to be incomplete. The fiesta is by nature sacred, literally or figuratively, and above all it is the advent of the unusual. It is governed by its own special rules, that set it apart from other days, and it has a logic, an ethic and even an economy that are often in conflict with everyday norms. It all occurs in an enchanted world: time is transformed to a mythical past or a total present; space, the scene of the fiesta, is turned into a gaily decorated world of its own; and the persons taking part cast off all human or social rank and become, for the moment, living images. And everything takes place as if it were not so, as if it were a dream. But whatever happens, our actions have a greater lightness, a different gravity. They take on other meanings and with them we contract new obligations. We throw down our burdens of time and reason.

In certain fiestas the very notion of order disappears. Chaos comes back and license rules. Anything is permitted: the customary hierarchies vanish, along with all social, sex, caste, and trade distinctions. Men disguise themselves as women, gentlemen as slaves, the poor as the rich. The army, the clergy, and the law are ridiculed. Obligatory sacrilege, ritual profanation is committed. Love becomes promiscuity. Sometimes the fiesta becomes a Black Mass. Regulations, habits and customs are violated. Respectable people put away the dignified expressions and conservative clothes that isolate them, dress up in gaudy colors, hide behind a mask, and escape from themselves.

Therefore the fiesta is not only an excess, a ritual squandering of the goods painfully accumulated during the rest of the year; it is also a revolt, a sudden immersion in the formless, in pure being. By means of the fiesta society frees itself from the norms it has established. It ridicules its gods, its principles, and its laws: it denies its own self.

10   The fiesta is a revolution in the most literal sense of the word. In the confusion that it generates, society is dissolved, is drowned, insofar as it is an organism ruled according to certain laws and principles. But it drowns in itself, in its own original chaos or liberty. Everything is united: good and evil, day and night, the sacred and the profane. Everything merges, loses shape and individuality and returns to the primordial mass. The fiesta is a cosmic experiment, an experiment in disorder, reuniting contradictory elements and principles in order to bring about a renascence of life. Ritual death promotes a rebirth; vomiting increases the appetite; the orgy, sterile in itself, renews the fertility of the mother or of the earth. The fiesta is a return to a remote and undifferentiated state, prenatal or presocial. It is a return that is also a beginning, in accordance with the dialectic that is inherent in social processes.

The group emerges purified and strengthened from this plunge into chaos. It has immersed itself in its own origins, in the womb from which it came. To express it in another way, the fiesta denies society as an organic system of differentiated forms and principles, but affirms it as a source of creative energy. It is a true "re-creation," the opposite of the "recreation" characterizing modern vacations, which do not entail any rites or ceremonies whatever and are as individualistic and sterile as the world that invented them.

Society communes with itself during the fiesta. Its members return to original chaos and freedom. Social structures break down and new relationships, unexpected rules, capricious hierarchies are created. In the general disorder everybody forgets himself and enters into otherwise forbidden situations and places. The bounds between audience and actors, officials and servants, are erased. Everybody takes part in the fiesta, everybody is caught up in its whirlwind. Whatever its mood, its character, its meaning, the fiesta is participation, and this trait distinguishes it from all other ceremonies and social phenomena. Lay or religious, orgy or saturnalia, the fiesta is a social act based on the full participation of all its celebrants.

Thanks to the fiesta the Mexican opens out, participates, communes with his fellows and with the values that give meaning to his religious or political existence. And it is significant that a country as sorrowful as ours should have so many and such joyous fiestas. Their frequency, their brilliance and excitement, the enthusiasm with which we take part, all suggest that without them we would explode. They free us, if only momentarily, from the thwarted impulses, the inflammable desires that we carry within us. But the Mexican fiesta is not merely a return to an original state of formless and normless liberty: the Mexican is not seeking to return, but to escape from himself, to exceed himself. Our fiestas are explosions. Life and death, joy and sorrow, music and mere noise are united, not to re-create or recognize themselves, but to swallow each other up. There is nothing so joyous as a Mexican fiesta, but there is also nothing so sorrowful. Fiesta night is also a night of mourning.

If we hide within ourselves in our daily lives, we discharge ourselves in the whirlwind of the fiesta. It is more than an opening out: we rend ourselves open. Everything—music, love, friendship—ends in tumult and violence. The frenzy of our festivals shows the extent to which our solitude closes us off from communication with the world. We are familiar with delirium, with songs and shouts, with the monologue . . . but not with the dialogue. Our fiestas, like our confidences, our loves, our attempts to reorder our society, are violent breaks with the old or the established. Each time we try to express ourselves we have to break with ourselves. And the fiesta is only one example, perhaps the most typical, of this violent break. It is not difficult to name others, equally revealing: our games, which are always going to extremes, often mortal; our profligate spending, the reverse of our timid investments and business enterprises; our confessions. The somber Mexican, closed up in himself, suddenly explodes, tears open his breast and reveals himself, though not without a certain complacency, and not without a stopping place in the shameful or terrible mazes of his intimacy. We are not frank, but our sincerity can reach extremes that horrify a European. The explosive, dramatic, sometimes even suicidal manner in which we strip

ourselves, surrender ourselves, is evidence that something in-
hibits and suffocates us. Something impedes us from being.
And since we cannot or dare not confront our own selves, we
resort to the fiesta. It fires us into the void; it is a drunken rap-
ture that burns itself out, a pistol shot in the air, a skyrocket.

The Initiation of
a Maasai Warrior

Tepilit Ole Saitoti

Born in 1949 in Lorkojita Albalbal, Tanzania, Tepilit Ole
Saitoti became the first to create an autobiographical account
(of which the following selection is a part) of his life as a
member of the Maasai, a cattle-herding community located in
and around the Great Rift Valley in Africa. Saitoti studied animal ecology in the United States and then returned to Kenya
to take part in the conservation projects concerning the Maasai land and people.

My Thoughts in Writing

1. Saitoti makes it clear that the Maasai male circumcision
   ceremony is actually a tradition of many traditions. What
   other traditions are practiced in preparation for the circumcision ceremony itself? How important are they? How
   do you know? Use the text to support your answer.
2. Although Saitoti's essay is primarily about the Maasai
   male circumcision ceremony and the traditions that go
   along with it, there is another distinct Maasai tradition
   mentioned in his account. What is that tradition? How is
   it related to the male circumcision tradition? How does it
   compare in significance to the Maasai male circumcision
   ceremony?
3. Saitoti explains that the Maasai male circumcision tradition is similar to the Christian baptism. Why do you think
   Saitoti mentions this similarity? What purpose does the

circumcision ceremony serve? What happens to the boys who go through it? How are they treated? What is expected of them? How does all of this affect them as individuals and as members of the Maasai community?

———————— ✦ ————————

Tepilit, circumcision means a sharp knife cutting into the skin of the most sensitive part of your body. You must not budge; don't move a muscle or even blink. You can face only one direction until the operation is completed. The slightest movement on your part will mean you are a coward, incompetent and unworthy to be a Maasai man. Ours has always been a proud family, and we would like to keep it that way. We will not tolerate unnecessary embarrassment, so you had better be ready. If you are not, tell us now so that we will not proceed. Imagine yourself alone remaining uncircumcised like the water youth [white people]. I hear they are not circumcised. Such a thing is not known in Maasailand; therefore, circumcision will have to take place even if it means holding you down until it is completed."

My father continued to speak and every one of us kept quiet. "The pain you will feel is symbolic. There is a deeper meaning in all this. Circumcision means a break between childhood and adulthood. For the first time in your life, you are regarded as a grownup, a complete man or woman. You will be expected to give and not just to receive. To protect the family always, not just to be protected yourself. And your wise judgment will for the first time be taken into consideration. No family affairs will be discussed without your being consulted. If you are ready for all these responsibilities, tell us now. Coming into manhood is not simply a matter of growth and maturity. It is a heavy load on your shoulders and especially a burden on the mind. Too much of this—I am done. I have said all I wanted to say. Fellows, if you have anything to add, go ahead and tell your brother, because I am through. I have spoken."

After a prolonged silence, one of my half-brothers said awkwardly, "Face it, man. . . it's painful. I won't lie about it, but it is not the end. We all went through it, after all. Only blood will flow, not milk." There was laughter and my father left.

My brother Lellia said, "Men, there are many things we must acquire and preparations we must make before the ceremony, and we will need the cooperation and help of all of you. Ostrich feathers for the crown and wax for the arrows must be collected."

5 "Are you *orkirekenyi?*" One of my brothers asked. I quickly replied no, and there was laughter. *Orkirekenyi* is a person who has transgressed sexually. For you must not have sexual intercourse with any circumcised woman before you yourself are circumcised. You must wait until you are circumcised. If you have not waited, you will be fined. Your father, mother, and the circumciser will take a cow from you as punishment.

Just before we departed, one of my closest friends said, "If you kick the knife, you will be in trouble." There was laughter. "By the way, if you have decided to kick the circumciser, do it well. Silence him once and for all." "Do it the way you kick a football in school." "That will fix him," another added, and we all laughed our heads off again as we departed.

The following month was a month of preparation. I and others collected wax, ostrich feathers, honey to be made into honey beer for the elders to drink on the day of circumcision, and all the other required articles.

Three days before the ceremony my head was shaved and I discarded all my belongings, such as my necklaces, garments, spear, and sword. I even had to shave my public hair. Circumcision in many ways is similar to Christian baptism. You must put all the sins you have committed during childhood behind and embark as a new person with a different outlook on a new life.

The circumciser came the following day and handed the ritual knives to me. He left drinking a calabash of beer. I stared at the knives uneasily. It was hard to accept that he was going to use them on my organ. I was to sharpen them and protect them from people of ill will who might try to blunt them, thus rendering them inefficient during the ritual and thereby bringing shame on our family. The knives threw a chill down my spine; I was not sure I was sharpening them properly, so I took them to my closest brother for him to check out, and he assured me that the knives were all right. I hid them well and waited.

Tension started building between me and my relatives, 10
most of whom worried that I wouldn't make it through the
ceremony valiantly. Some even snarled at me, which was
their way of encouraging me. Others threw insults and abu-
sive words my way. My sister Loiyan in particular was more
troubled by the whole affair than anyone in the whole family. She had to assume my mother's role during the circumcision. Were I to fail my initiation, she would have to face
the consequences. She would be spat upon and even beaten
for representing the mother of an unworthy son. The same
fate would befall my father, but he seemed unconcerned. He
had this weird belief that because I was not particularly
handsome, I must be brave. He kept saying, "God is not so
bad as to have made him ugly and a coward at the same
time."

Failure to be brave during circumcision would have other
unfortunate consequences: the herd of cattle belonging to the
family still in the compound would be beaten until they stam-
peded; the slaughtered oxen and honey beer prepared during
the month before the ritual would go to waste; the initiate's
food would be spat upon and he would have to eat it or else
get a severe beating. Everyone would call him Olkasiodoi, the
knife kicker.

Kicking the knife of the circumciser would not help you
anyway. If you struggle and try to get away during the ritual,
you will be held down until the operation is completed. Such
failure of nerve would haunt you in the future. For example,
no one will choose a person who kicked the knife for a position of leadership. However, there have been instances in
which a person who failed to go through circumcision suc-
cessfully became very brave afterwards because he was filled
with anger over the incident; no one dares to scold him or remind him of it. His agemates, particularly the warriors, will
act as if nothing had happened.

During the circumcision of a woman, on the other hand,
she is allowed to cry as long as she does not hinder the operation. It is common to see a woman crying and kicking during
circumcision. Warriors are usually summoned to help hold
her down.

For women, circumcision means an end to the company of Maasai warriors. After they recuperate, they soon get married, and often to men twice their age.

15   The closer it came to the hour of truth, the more I was hated, particularly by those closest to me. I was deeply troubled by the withdrawal of all the support I needed. My annoyance turned into anger and resolve. I decided not to budge or blink, even if I were to see my intestines flowing before me. My resolve was hardened when newly circumcised warriors came to sing for me. Their songs were utterly insulting, intended to annoy me further. They tucked their wax arrows under my crotch and rubbed them on my nose. They repeatedly called me names.

By the end of the singing, I was fuming. Crying would have meant I was a coward. After midnight they left me alone and I went into the house and tried to sleep but could not. I was exhausted and numb but remained awake all night.

At dawn I was summoned once again by the newly circumcised warriors. They piled more and more insults on me. They sang their weird songs with even more vigor and excitement than before. The songs praised warriorhood and encouraged one to achieve it at all costs. The songs continued until the sun shone on the cattle horns clearly. I was summoned to the main cattle gate, in my hand a ritual cowhide from a cow that had been properly slaughtered during my naming ceremony. I went past Loiyan, who was milking a cow, and she muttered something. She was shaking all over. There was so much tension that people could hardly breathe.

I laid the hide down and a boy was ordered to pour ice-cold water, known as *engare entolu* (ax water), over my head. It dripped all over my naked body and I shook furiously. In a matter of seconds. I was summoned to sit down. A large crowd of boys and men formed a semicircle in front of me; women are not allowed to watch male circumcision and vice versa. That was the last thing I saw clearly. As soon as I sat down, the circumciser appeared, his knives at the ready. He spread my legs and said, "One cut," a pronouncement necessary to prevent an initiate from claiming that he had been taken by surprise. He splashed a white liquid, a ceremonial paint called *enturoto*, across my face. Almost immediately I felt a spark of pain under my belly as the knife cut through my penis' foreskin. I happened to choose to look in the direction of the operation. I continued to observe the circumciser's fingers working mechanically. The pain became numbness and my lower body felt heavy, as if I were weighed down by a heavy burden. After fifteen minutes or so, a man who had been supporting from behind pointed at something, as if to assist the circumciser. I came to learn later that the circumciser's eyesight had been failing him and that my brothers had been mad at him because the operation had taken longer than was usually necessary. All the same, I remained pinned down until the operation was over. I heard a call for milk to wash the knives, which signaled the end, and soon the ceremony was over.

With words of praise, I was told to wake up, but I remained seated. I waited for the customary presents in appreciation of my bravery. My father gave me a cow and so did my brother Lellia. The man who had supported my back and my brother-in-law gave me a heifer. In all I had eight animals given to me. I was carried inside the house to my own bed to recuperate as activities intensified to celebrate my bravery.

I laid on my own bed and bled profusely. The blood must be retained within the bed, for according to Maasai tradition, it must not spill to the ground. I was drenched in my own blood. I stopped bleeding after about half an hour but soon was in intolerable pain. I was supposed to squeeze my organ and force blood to flow out of the wound, but no one had told me, so the blood coagulated and caused unbearable pain. The circumciser was brought to my aid and showed me what to do, and soon the pain subsided.

The following morning, I was escorted by a small boy to a nearby valley to walk and relax, allowing my wound to drain. This was common for everyone who had been circumcised, as well as for women who had just given birth. Having lost a lot of blood, I was extremely weak. I walked very slowly, but in spite of my caution I fainted. I tried to hang on to bushes and shrubs, but I fell, irritating my wound. I came out of unconsciousness quickly, and the boy who was escorting me never realized what had happened. I was so scared that I told him to lead me back home. I could have died without there being anyone around who could have helped me. From that day on, I was selective of my company while I was feeble.

In two weeks I was able to walk and was taken to join other newly circumcised boys far away from our settlement. By tradition Maasai initiates are required to decorate their headdresses with all kinds of colorful birds they have killed. On our way to the settlement, we hunted birds and teased girls by shooting them with our wax blunt arrows. We danced and ate and were well treated wherever we went. We were protected from the cold and rain during the healing period. We were not allowed to touch food, as we were regarded as unclean, so whenever we ate we had to use specially prepared sticks instead. We remained in this pampered state until our wounds healed and our headdresses were removed. Our heads were shaved, we discarded our black cloaks and bird headdresses and embarked as newly shaven warriors, Irkeleani.

As long as I live I will never forget the day my head was shaved and I emerged a man, a Maasai warrior. I felt a sense of control over my destiny so great that no words can accurately describe it. I now stood with confidence, pride, and happiness of being, for all around me I was desired and loved by beautiful, sensuous Maasai maidens. I could now interact with women and even have sex with them, which I had not been allowed before. I was now regarded as a responsible person.

In the old days, warriors were like gods, and women and men wanted only to be the parent of a warrior. Everything else would be taken care of as a result. When a poor family had a warrior, they ceased to be poor. The warrior would go on raids and bring cattle back. The warrior would defend the family against all odds. When a society respects the individual and displays confidence in him the way the Maasai do their warriors, the individual can grow to his fullest potential. Whenever there was a task requiring physical strength or bravery, the Maasai would call upon their warriors. They hardly ever fall short of what is demanded of them and so are characterized by pride, confidence, and an extreme sense of freedom. But there is an old saying in Maasai: "You are never a free man until your father dies." In other words, your father is paramount while he is alive and you are obligated to respect him. My father took advantage of this principle and held a tight grip on all his warriors, including myself. He always wanted to know where we all were at any given time. We fought against his restrictions, but without success. I, being the youngest of my father's five warriors, tried even harder to get loose repeatedly, but each time I was punished severely.

Roaming the plains with other warriors in pursuit of girls   25
and adventure was a warrior's pastime. We would wander from one settlement to another, singing, wrestling, hunting, and just playing. Often I was ready to risk my father's punishment for this wonderful freedom.

One clear day my father sent me to take sick children and one of his wives to the dispensary in the Korongoro Highlands. We rode in the L. S. B. Leakey lorry. We ascended the highlands and were soon attended to in the local hospital. Near the conservation offices I met several acquaintances, and one of them told me of an unusual circumcision that was about to take place in a day or two. All the local warriors and girls were preparing to attend it.

The highlands were a lush green from the seasonal rains and the sky was a purple-blue with no clouds in sight. The land was overflowing with milk, and the warriors felt and looked their best, as they always did when there was plenty to eat and drink. Everyone was at ease. The demands the community usually made on warriors during the dry season when water was scarce and wells had to be dug were now not necessary. Herds and flocks were entrusted to youths to look after. The warriors had all the time for themselves. But my father was so strict that even at times like these he still insisted on overworking us in one way or another. He believed that by keeping us busy, he would keep us out of trouble.

When I heard about the impending ceremony, I decided to remain behind in the Korongoro Highlands and attend it now that the children had been treated. I knew very well that I would have to make up a story for my father upon my return, but I would worry about that later. I had left my spear at home when I boarded the bus, thinking that I would be coming back that very day. I felt lighter but now regretted having left it behind; I was so used to carrying it wherever I went. In gales of laughter resulting from our continuous teasing of each other, we made our way toward a distant kraal. We walked at a leisurely pace and reveled in the breeze. As usual we talked about the women we desired, among other things.

The following day we were joined by a long line of colorfully dressed girls and warriors from the kraal and the neighborhood where we had spent the night, and we left the highland and headed to Ingorienito to the rolling hills on the lower slopes to attend the circumcision ceremony. From there one could see Oldopai Gorge, where my parents lived, and the Inaapi hills in the middle of the Serengeti Plain.

30   Three girls and a boy were to be initiated on the same day, an unusual occasion. Four oxen were to be slaughtered, and many people would therefore attend. As we descended, we saw the kraal where the ceremony would take place. All those people dressed in red seemed from a distance like flamingos standing in a lake. We could see lines of other guests heading to the settlements. Warriors made gallant cries of happiness known as *enkiseer*. Our line of warriors and girls responded to their cries even more gallantly.

In serpentine fashion, we entered the gates of the settlement. Holding spears in our left hands, we warriors walked proudly, taking small steps, swaying like palm trees, impressing our girls, who walked parallel to us in another line, and of course the spectators, who gazed at us approvingly.

We stopped in the center of the kraal and waited to be greeted. Women and children welcomed us. We put our hands on the children's heads, which is how children are commonly saluted. After the greetings were completed, we started dancing.

Our singing echoed off the kraal fence and nearby trees. Another line of warriors came up the hill and entered the compound, also singing and moving slowly toward us. Our singing grew in intensity. Both lines of warriors moved parallel to each other, and our feet pounded the ground with style. We stamped vigorously, as if to tell the next line and the spectators that we were the best.

The singing continued until the hot sun was overhead. We recessed and ate food already prepared for us by other warriors. Roasted meat was for those who were to eat meat, and milk for the others. By our tradition, meat and milk must not be consumed at the same time, for this would be a betrayal of the animal. It was regarded as cruel to consume a product of the animal that could be obtained while it was alive, such as milk, and meat, which was only available after the animal had been killed.

After eating we resumed singing, and I spotted a tall, beau-   35
tiful *esiankiki* (young maiden) of Masiaya whose family was one of the largest and richest in our area. She stood very erect and seemed taller than the rest.

One of her breasts could be seen just above her dress, which was knotted at the shoulder. While I was supposed to dance generally to please all the spectators, I took it upon myself to please her especially. I stared at and flirted with her, and she and I danced in unison at times. We complemented each other very well.

During a break, I introduced myself to the *esiankiki* and told her I would like to see her after the dance. "Won't you need a warrior to escort you home later when the evening threatens?" I said. She replied, "Perhaps, but the evening is still far away."

I waited patiently. When the dance ended, I saw her departing with a group of other women her age. She gave me a sidelong glance, and I took that to mean come later and not now. With so many others around, I would not have been able to confer with her as I would have liked anyway.

With another warrior, I wandered around the kraal killing time until the herds returned from pasture. Before the sun dropped out of sight, we departed. As the kraal of the *esiankiki* was in the lowlands, a place called Enkoloa, we descended leisurely, our spears resting on our shoulders.

We arrived at the woman's kraal and found that cows were   40
now being milked. One could hear the women trying to appease the cows by singing to them. Singing calms cows down, making it easier to milk them. There were no warriors in the whole kraal except for the two of us. Girls went around into

warriors' houses as usual and collected milk for us. I was so eager to go and meet my *esiankiki* that I could hardly wait for nightfall. The warriors' girls were trying hard to be sociable, but my mind was not with them. I found them to be childish, loud, bothersome, and boring.

As the only warriors present, we had to keep them company and sing for them, at least for a while, as required by custom. I told the other warrior to sing while I tried to figure out how to approach my *esiankiki*. Still a novice warrior, I was not experienced with women and was in fact still afraid of them. I could flirt from a distance, of course. But sitting down with a woman and trying to seduce her was another matter. I had already tried twice to approach women soon after my circumcision and had failed. I got as far as the door of one woman's house and felt my heart beating like a Congolese drum; breathing became difficult and I had to turn back. Another time I managed to get in the house and succeeded in sitting on the bed, but then I started trembling until the whole bed was shaking, and conversation became difficult. I left the house and the woman, amazed and speechless, and never went back to her again.

Tonight I promised myself I would be brave and would not make any silly, ridiculous moves. "I must be mature and not afraid," I kept reminding myself, as I remembered an incident involving one of my relatives when he was still very young and, like me, afraid of women. He went to a woman's house and sat on a stool for a whole hour; he was afraid to awaken her, as his heart was pounding and he was having difficulty breathing.

When he finally calmed down, he woke her up, and their conversation went something like this:

"Woman, wake up."
45   "Why should I?"
"To light the fire."
"For what?"
"So you can see me."
"I already know who you are. Why don't *you* light the fire, as you're nearer to it than me?"
50   "It's your house and it's only proper that you light it yourself."
"I don't feel like it."

"At least wake up so we can talk, as I have something to tell you."

"Say it."

"I need you."

"I do not need one-eyed types like yourself."   55

"One-eyed people are people too."

"That might be so, but they are not to my taste."

They continued talking for quite some time, and the more they spoke, the braver he became. He did not sleep with her that night, but later on he persisted until he won her over. I doubted whether I was as strong-willed as he, but the fact that he had met with success encouraged me. I told my warrior friend where to find me should he need me, and then I departed.

When I entered the house of my *esiankiki*, I called for the woman of the house, and as luck would have it, my lady responded. She was waiting for me. I felt better, and I proceeded to talk to her like a professional. After much talking back and forth, I joined her in bed.

The night was calm, tender, and loving, like most nights   60
after initiation ceremonies as big as this one. There must have been a lot of courting and lovemaking.

Maasai women can be very hard to deal with sometimes. They can simply reject a man outright and refuse to change their minds. Some play hard to get, but in reality are testing the man to see whether he is worth their while. Once a friend of mine while still young was powerfully attracted to a woman nearly his mother's age. He put a bold move on her. At first the woman could not believe his intention, or rather was amazed by his courage. The name of the warrior was Ngengeiya, or Drizzle.

"Drizzle, what do you want?"

The warrior stared her right in the eye and said, "You."

"For what?"

"To make love to you."   65

"I am your mother's age."

"The choice was either her or you."

This remark took the woman by surprise. She had underestimated the saying "There is no such thing as a young warrior." When you are a warrior, you are expected to perform bravely in any situation. Your age and size are immaterial.

"You mean you could really love me like a grownup man?"

70 "Try me, woman."

He moved in on her. Soon the woman started moaning with excitement, calling out his name. "Honey Drizzle, Honey Drizzle, you *are* a man." In a breathy, stammering voice, she said, "A real man."

Her attractiveness made Honey Drizzle ignore her relative old age. The Maasai believe that if an older and a younger person have intercourse, it is the older person who stands to gain. For instance, it is believed that an older woman having an affair with a young man starts to appear younger and healthier, while the young man grows older and unhealthy.

The following day when the initiation rites had ended, I decided to return home. I had offended my father by staying away from home without his consent, so I prepared myself for whatever punishment he might inflict on me. I walked home alone.

Taxidermist's Funeral

Andrew Rein

Andrew Rein was born in New York City in 1970. His parents passed to him a mixed religious heritage, one he often comments on in his writing. The following selection reflects his parents' efforts to instill tradition in the young Andrew without truly understanding it themselves.

My Thoughts in Writing

1. In the introduction, Rein tells us that "traditions never seemed important enough" for him to look at. What, if anything, do you think he learns about the value of tradition from his uncle's funeral? How do you know? Use the text to support your answer.

2. What does his uncle's funeral have to do with the essay's final statement? Do you agree or disagree with the conclusion Rein comes to about traditions? Provide examples from your own life to support your answer.

3. What aspects of the funeral tradition does Rein question? What types of answers does he receive? Are they sufficient? Why or why not?

———————— ✦ ————————

Traditions are not things that I've ever looked at in my family much less in myself. It's not that I considered them old fashioned or boring. They never seemed important enough to me to look at.

When I was ten years old, my Uncle Charlie died. He was the first person I had known who had died. I wasn't close to him, so when it happened I didn't feel a sense of loss, hurt or wanting to cry. The only memories I have of him are of going to his shop: Uncle Charlie was a taxidermist. When I would enter the shop, I would be overwhelmed by the pungent odor of formaldehyde; stuffed animals on wooden stands stared out at me with glass eyes. "Some man," my mom said about my uncle. He would pat me on the head with an old wrinkled hand and tell me through an old wrinkled mouth clinching a cigar, what a good boy I was.

One morning, my mom came into my room sobbing. "Uncle Charlie is dead." Two days later I was in a big, dark, creepy funeral home. My father came up to me with a yarmulka and put it on my head. "What is this for?" I questioned. "Tradition," he answered, "just wear it." I left it on my head and didn't think anything else of it.

The next memory I have of that day is standing in front of the open coffin, looking at my pale green, clammy looking, dead Uncle Charlie. "I thought they were supposed to make you look alive when you are dead," I thought to myself. He didn't look alive at all; not like the stuffed animals on wooden stands that stared with glass eyes. Uncle Charlie looked dead.

The ride to the cemetery was long and hot since the air 5 conditioner was broken, and we couldn't open the windows more than a crack because the breeze would mess up my mother's hair. She was wearing a torn piece of cloth pinned to her lapel. "What's that for?" I asked pointing to the cloth. "When somebody close to you dies," she answered, "you tear a piece of your clothing as a sign of respect at the loss of a family member." "So why the cloth?" I asked. "Because this outfit was very expensive," she answered.

The rest of the day, the eulogy, the burial, is a blur. The only other memory I have of the event is getting a stuffed squirrel three weeks later.

Although traditions are not emphasized in my house, they're there and alive, just waiting for something to stir them from their sleep and come to us, unexpectedly.

Meaning of hunt lost from afar
Nicole Brodeur

A graduate of Rowan University in Glassboro, New Jersey, Nicole Brodeur, 41, has written for such newspapers as the *Philadelphia Inquirer*, the *Orange Country* (CA) *Resister*, the *Seattle Times*, and the Raleigh, North Carolina, *News and Observer*. An acute observer of everyday life, Brodeur's work covers social issues, politics, and general human interest stories. In 1995, Brodeur took first place for humorous columns from the North Carolina Press Association, and in 1998 she won first place in the National Headliner Award Competition.

My Thoughts in Writing

1. During her experience, Brodeur encounters more than one endangered thing. Like the gray whales, what does she learn is also in danger of extinction?
2. In what ways is the Makah tribe served by the whale hunt tradition? What happened to the tribe when whaling became illegal?
3. Brodeur tells us that "two generations of Makahs never had a chance to see the traditional way to whale." In her opinion, how has this affected the present hunt? Is her Thanksgiving comparison effective in helping you understand the effects she sees? Why or why not? How do mem-

bers of the tribe feel about the renewal of this ancient tradition, about the killing of the gray whales?

———————— ✦ ————————

If we are a nation that truly "celebrates" diversity, then this week the Makah reservation was a proving ground—a party that tests the depths of our acceptance.

Watching the hunt of a gray whale from our comfy homes in Seattle, it was easy to be outraged by the bloodshed and the cheering.

But there had to be something more at the heart of what seemed like senseless murder.

So I drove to Neah Bay, at the far corner of the country, where this ramshackle community sits like a bedsheet that won't stay tucked under—a lack of order that somehow offends a lot of us.

By the time I arrived, the whale was just a bloody carcass. 5 A sour smell hung in the air. Kids jiggled the flesh with sticks. Blood-caked knives still sat in the cedar-bark canoes.

I was searching for spirit, but saw only spoils.

Then a group of men circled the remains, chanting and drumming.

I heard a voice behind me: "That's so the soul of the whale will rest in peace," whispered Janet Elofson, 38, a Makah now living in Port Angeles.

When the drumming ended, there was silence, save for the grinding of the TV trucks that lined the road.

"His spirit has gone now, to his ancestors," said drummer 10 Spencer McCarty, 39, stepping back from the circle. "It's an expression of respect."

It was a respect I had missed from afar.

The hunt offers the tribe a chance to transform the future, McCarty said; it was healing to honor the traditions of the past.

"That part of it has been a really positive influence for a lot of people," McCarty said.

The tribe started to fracture when whaling was outlawed in the 1920s. The culture crumbled even more in 1930, when the U.S. government forced Makah families to dismantle their longhouses, saying that communal living was against the law.

15   Crime and drug problems set in, McCarty said, as members lost their spiritual mooring.

Perhaps the Makahs needed an act as profound as this kill to end their 70-year cultural coma.

The problem is that in that same time, whales became hallowed creatures to the rest of us—the revered subject of murals, museum exhibits, even the ballads of Crosby, Stills and Nash.

And the Makahs, strangely, became more like us.

So of course whalers called in the kill on a cell phone. Of course they stood atop the whale as it was hauled into the bay, arms stabbing at the sky, a visual echo of Monday Night Football.

20   Two generations of Makahs never had a chance to see the traditional way to whale. Imagine a young boy trying to carve the Thanksgiving turkey like his grandfather did, when his father never learned.

Yes, the hunt was violent and bloody. It made schoolchildren cry. It made me sick.

But it made Kathryn Gyori, a 14-year-old Makah, proud.

"People don't understand what being native really is," she told me. "You can't understand this feeling. The tribe is getting back to the old ways of its ancestors. . . . I feel peaceful."

Consider this: As long as the whales were endangered, so was the heart of the Makahs. We should not judge what we can't understand.

25   "We will be the last people to want whales not to survive," McCarty said.

"Because whatever happens to them will happen to us, too."

Sample Student Essay

My Family Traditions

LISA DESJARDINS

When I was first asked what traditions my family has, I found it hard to think of any. When I thought of traditions, I could only think of big events, such as family reunions or Sunday dinners with the whole family. Because my extended family lives so far away, I haven't had a chance to experience those celebrations or regular gatherings. Still, I knew that since even small everyday or large every year recurring events can be traditions, there must be some kind of tradition in which my immediate family engaged. After all, sometimes it is the most seemingly insignificant things we do together on a regular basis that have the most meaning.

My family (my mom, my dad, and me) has many small traditions that we have carried on for years. For instance, we eat dinner as a family at 6:30 every night. We have been doing that for so long that it feels awkward if we don't. Another thing my family does together on a regular basis is chores. Saturday is the day my mom sets aside for the whole family to work together around the house. In addition, it used to be when I was little, I had a bedtime of eight o'clock. Before I went to bed, my mom would come tuck me in and read to me. She did that until I was ten years old. As I think of all of the small traditions that my family had and still has, I also think about some of the bigger traditions in which we engage.

Every year my family comes together to celebrate the holidays. The first thing that we do to get ready for the holidays is put the decorations up. Used to be, we would just pick a day in advance and everyone would need to be home that day to help. Now that I am older, my parents are a little more lenient about letting me do my own thing, but when I was little, we always decorated together. Two holidays that we do this for that stick out in my mind the clearest are Halloween and Christmas.

When I was younger, every year in October, in celebration of the coming Halloween holiday, my parents and I would go to Johnson's Farm to pick out a pumpkin. We would go on the hay ride out to the pumpkin patch and find just the right one. When we were done, we would go back to the farm and buy a dozen of Johnson's apple cider donuts and bring them home to eat. Later on that day, we would do the job of making the jack-o'-lantern. After we had the jack-o'-lantern looking just right, my dad would toast the pumpkinseeds and we would eat them.

Christmas was another big holiday for us when I was a little girl, and it still is; not much has changed. Every year, two weeks before Christmas, my family gets the tree ready. My dad puts on the Christmas music and we bring all of the Christmas decorations in from the garage. When we have everything up, including all of the outside lights, we relax near the fireplace with hot chocolate and cookies.

When the Halloween and Christmas holidays finally come, my family has more traditions. When I was little, Halloween was my favorite holiday. My parents always let me pick out a great costume and then came the trick-or-treating time. They would take me around the neighborhood, and I wasn't allowed to have any candy until I got home. My parents would then check the candy for dangerous items and once they okayed everything, I could indulge myself. While I truly loved that holiday as a kid, now that I am older, Halloween has taken a back seat in my heart to Christmas.

These days, Christmas is my favorite holiday, for it is all about our traditions. My parents always get me up early on Christmas morning to open gifts. After that, my parents make a big breakfast that usually consists of scrambled eggs and cheese, bacon, toast with butter and jelly, and fried potatoes. After we finish eating and we clean up all the dishes, we start calling my aunts, uncles, and grandparents. When we are through with that, my parents and I get ready to prepare Christmas dinner. My mother sets out all the good china in the dining room, while my father and I start preparing the food. Our dinner usually consists of ham, crescent rolls, my mother's homemade mashed potatoes, and her green beans. For dessert, my dad always makes hot homemade apple pie with vanilla ice cream and a variety of Christmas cookies. After my parents and I are finished eating, we begin to clean up the kitchen and the dining room. I help my mom hand wash the china, while my dad puts the leftovers away. When the kitchen and dining room are spotless, my dad picks out a movie on the television for us to watch while we relax and our food digests.

Traditions are a large part of my family. I did not really see that until now. Traditions are something that I look forward to and something that I would be lost without. It is nice to have so many things that we do the same way every day or year after year. Over time things change with our traditions, but the final outcome is always the same. My family's traditions are about being with each other and enjoying ourselves. Like the traditions of so many other families, they are all about togetherness.

My Thoughts in Writing

1. In the beginning of her essay, Desjardins shares with her readers her original belief that she had no traditions in her family. Why do you think she shares this information with you? What brings her to the realization that her family does have traditions?

2. How important are Desjardins's traditions to her and the other members of her family? How do you know? Provide evidence from the text to support your answer.

3. What are the traditions Desjardins outlines in this essay? Are they all of the same type or do they differ? How?

The Readings Come Together

1. Compare the introductions and conclusions to the essays by Desjardins and Rein. How are their initial and concluding points similar? Which writer does a better job of connecting the body of the essay to the essay's conclusion? Use evidence from the essays to help you make your point.

2. The essays by Vergara and Paz are both about festivals—Italian and Mexican, respectively. What common social purpose do both Vergara and Paz at-

tribute to the festivals of their ancestral homelands? What do southern Italy and Mexico have in common that makes them perfect settings for frequent festivals?

3. The traditions in the essays by Saitoti and Brodeur are quite controversial. Study both essays to determine what the controversy is surrounding each tradition and how the controversies are similar. Is either author trying to justify the tradition despite the controversy surrounding it? If so, state which author and how. Use the text to clarify your point.

4. The writers in this chapter present a number of unique traditions. List all the traditions discussed and then identify which ones you are familiar with and which ones you are not. In what ways are your traditions similar to the ones you have read about in this chapter? How are they different? What do you learn by studying the various traditions of other people?

5. A number of the essays are about traditions that are either threatened or that have already died out. From the list you created earlier, divide the traditions into the following categories: alive and well, threatened, or died out. Why do you think some traditions have survived and others have not? What things can threaten traditions? What can be done to keep traditions alive?

There's Something More out There

Part I

At-Home Activity

Prelude Prewriting.   In your journal, create a list of the traditional gatherings your family or community engages in annually. Your list might include birthdays, holidays, reunions, clambakes, vacations, Sunday dinners, Fourth of July picnics, summer block parties, church carnivals, and so forth. Then, identify which traditions are new and which are old. If a tradition is threatened, identify it as such and explain why this is the case. If a tradition has changed dramatically in your opinion, explain the change and whether you think it is good or bad and why.

Part II

Classroom Storytelling Session

Use your traditions to teach others about yourself. On the board, make a list of the many traditions your class discovered while working on the above. Then, discuss how each tradition is unique and what these traditions have in common.

Part III

Journal Entry

Take yourself through a year or month in the life of your family or community. Outline each of the traditions engaged in as the year or month progresses. Or, focusing on one specific year, outline the traditions your family or community engaged in as events specific to that year occurred: births, deaths, graduations, engagements, weddings, promotions, whatever.

Part IV

Writing Assignment

Using a brief analysis of one of the reading selections as a way of approaching your subject, create an essay providing examples of the many traditions specific to your family or community. These family- or community-specific traditions may be stylized traditions (that is, reshapings of traditions common to other families or communities), traditions solely of your family's or community's own creation (specific day-of-the-week dinners, yearly reunions, vacations, football parties, block parties), and/or traditions based on or drawn from your family's or community's background. Your essay's purpose is to get to the heart of the value of your traditions. Do these traditions keep you connected? Do they structure the passing years, providing you with a sense of security and stability? Does your family or community engage in traditions primarily to recognize accomplishments, to remember important dates, to pay tribute to important members, or simply to celebrate family or community? In other words, what purposes do your traditions serve, and, therefore, why is it important that the traditions be kept alive?

Traditional Processes

THE FOLKLORE FOCUS

The Process of Tradition

Shortly after the typical school year begins, the class and dorm room supplies lining the sale aisles of the nearby department stores are replaced by bags of candy, monster masks, witch hats, and rubber spiders. It takes but one trip around town to determine that, for the most part, Halloween is alive and well. The actual day is still weeks away and yet the preparations for the tradition are obvious and ongoing: jack-o'-lanterns have been carved and placed on doorsteps; front yards have been transformed into ancient, haunted cemeteries; gruesome costumes have been imagined, created, rented, or bought; and so on. All Hallows Eve comes and goes in the blink of an eye, yet what fun so many of us have in the process of getting ready for it. Whether it is a national, religious, family, or community celebration, isn't this pretty much the way of things? All we do in preparation for a tradition is part and parcel of what makes it so special. In other words, the process of the tradition is just as important as the tradition itself. After all, we couldn't have one (well, not the way we really wanted it to be) without the other.

The relevance of the process of a tradition is not new to folklorists. For quite some time, we have been interested in what it takes to create folklore or bring it about and how that process affects not only the product itself, but also those involved in its creation. Moreover, the interest in process applies not only to traditions that result in material products (such as baking, quilting, woodworking, decoy carving), but custom-related traditions (such as festivals, holidays, family gatherings), and traditional activities, tasks, or responsibilities (those things, such as housework or yard work that produce a rather intangible product). Whether it be the neighbor who carves birds so real you'd think they could fly, the community that fashions a festival so grand you wouldn't miss it for the world, or the mother who produces a floor so clean "you could eat off it," it is likely that the process engaged in during the course of creation was just as important as the product created.

Because who we are is so thoroughly tied up in what we do, studying the processes of our traditions can help us better understand the role folklore plays in our lives—as individuals and as family and/or community members. As mentioned in Chapter 3, folklore is one of the ways through which we forge our identities and make ourselves known to others. Indeed, many people engage in folklore as a way to better know themselves. For instance, my former neighbor was a woodworker. His basement was filled with the tools of his trade and evidence of his hard work. Once he took me down to his workshop so that he could retrieve the pepper grinder and pen sets he had made for me. At first, he stood modestly by as I admired the work of his hands, the fruits of his labor. Then, as we chatted about the candleholders he was fashioning from scraps of larger projects, he began to explain the purpose of his work. He said, "Here I figure things out, put things together. I can make something new from something old, and something old, much better." In the way his hands touched the wood and the machinery surrounding us, it was clear to me that his words applied to more than the objects he created. His folklore engagement was his way of working through the knotholes of life, of his life. It was not so much about the things he could make as it was about what the making provided—a kind of sustenance for the soul.

What traditional processes do you or your family/community members use to maneuver through life, to navigate the world? What do the processes of your traditions reveal about your values, your experiences, and your choices? This chapter encourages you to study the role of process in the creation of folk objects, customs, or activities, especially as it relates to personal or family/community identity. The readings selected for this chapter and the questions that follow them will help you do this. Each selection highlights the significance of a traditional process to those involved, and together they illustrate the value of this aspect of folklore engagement. The questions that precede each selection require you to further analyze the readings, to examine traditional processes, and to compare the purposes they serve and the way they are viewed. Writing about a process requires paying special attention to each step involved and to the significance of those steps as they contribute to the meaning of the process itself. As you study the selections and compare them to each other, make note of the way the writers use specific—and often step-by-step—sensory details to help you follow the process they are recalling. Your analysis of each reading's theme regarding the traditional process illustrated will help you focus on the importance of the process you choose to study and prepare you to convey that meaning in writing.

Seeing the Lush, Fresh Countryside Through City Eyes

Susan Jennifer Polese

Susan Jennifer Polese has written extensively about theater for *The Advocate, The Journal News,* and *The New York Times.* She is a member of The Dramatist Guild and has taught playwriting to children and young adults. Her own full-length play, *Klaus' Closet,* was produced Off-Broadway by The American Theatre for Actors at the Beckmann Theatre, and subsequently at the Westbeth Artists' Residency in New York City in 1993. Her play *After A Night with Abe* was produced in 1998 as part of the One-Act Festival at the Herbert Mark Newman Theatre in Pleasantville, New York.

My Thoughts in Writing

1. What is traditional about the process Polese describes in the essay? To what degree and in what ways have things changed since Polese first encountered this tradition? How have the changes affected her experience? Use the text to illustrate your answer.

2. Where in the essay does Polese explain the purpose of this traditional process? What does she gain from it and what does she suggest others will gain as well?

3. Polese describes in great detail the places she visits during her road trip. Why is it important that she do this? What does she find in these places? How are these places related to the type of trip she is taking?

———————— ✦ ————————

ON a bright Sunday morning my cousin Anthony and I jumped in his car and took a drive up Route 22, getting on the thoroughfare just south of Brewster and ending up far north in Columbia County.

It felt right to be chauffeured in this manner, especially by a male relative. Over the years I have made many a Route 22 road trip, initially in the early 1970's as one of three passengers in the back seat of my parents' 1965 Nash Rambler station wagon.

En route to my grandparents' summer home, my father always drove as my mother road shotgun. To the AM radio sounds of Blood, Sweat & Tears and the Jackson Five my family cruised north.

My brothers and I would roll down the windows to get a whiff of freshly cut grass, or to watch the cows peacefully grazing. We even savored the pungent odor of manure because it signaled our arrival in "the country."

5   Things had changed a little on my recent trip with Anthony. For one thing, I enjoyed an adult's front seat. But we were both giddy with anticipation. There were places to discover, people to meet.

One notable sight to be seen on Route 22 is Rosemary's Texas Taco. The eclectic sense of style of the proprietor, Rosemary Jamison, permeates this funky restaurant both inside and out. A native Texan, Ms. Jamison began her food service career in the late '60's, decked out as a cowgirl tending a Mexican food cart in front of the Plaza Hotel in Manhattan. In 1972 she opened her restaurant in the upper Hudson Valley.

Packed solid with actual memorabilia—not the prefabricated kind found in franchised restaurants—Rosemary's Texas Taco is an exploding collage of pop culture featuring outside seating and an affordable menu of Mexican tidbits. When you go, seat yourself in the back room, converse with a chatty parrot, and gaze at kitschy portraits of celebrities hung in gilded frames.

By the time you have passed this culinary haunt, as well as the Red Rooster Drive-In and Miniature Golf Course in Brewster and several authentic metal diners that serve breakfast at any time of day, you are well on your way to a major destination of this journey: Millerton. Founded in the mid-1800's and named after a civil engineer, Sidney G. Miller, Millerton is about as peaceful a burg as you'll find. Main Street is both charming and dotted with wonderful spots, including Simmons' Way Inn, which offers elegant overnight accommodations. Named after E. W. Simmons, a prominent statesman, educator and lawyer who built the original mansion in 1854, the house had an incarnation as a doctor's residence before it was renovated into an inn in 1903. The intimate hotel has a restaurant, but the most terrific thing is what a guest will discover within walking distance.

Across from Simmons' Way Inn is a first-run movie house with an intact balcony, a colorful thrift shop, a well-stocked bookstore and the hard-to describe Terni's. Philip Terni is the third generation of Terni men to tend this shop, which brings back days-of-yore untarnished. The soda fountain is fully functional, and when asked about store hours the shopkeeper says, "If the light's on, we're open." Terni's specializes in imported and domestic tackle as well as hunting supplies, which Mr. Terni supplements with candy, clothing and an admirable selection of magazines. Several yards away is Millerton Antique Center, housing more than 25 dealers under one roof. Just north of Millerton, Taconic State Park stretches across Route 22, and a right turn off the main drag takes you to scenic Rudd Pond Campground. Named after

Maj. Bezaleel Rudd, a commander in the American Revolution, the park is a serene place to take a dip or camp. There is a sandy swimming beach, fishing, a boat launch and rentals, a picnic grove and a children's campground, all framed by lush woodlands.

10   Taconic State Park is also home to Bash-Bish Falls, one of the most scenic waterfalls on the East Coast. Situated where Massachusetts, New York and Connecticut meet, the glistening falls tumble through a 200-foot gorge and cascade more than 60 feet into a deep boulder-lined pool. An easy trail leads the way to the top where a hiker can walk over three state lines in consecutive steps. Open dawn to dusk, with no admission, the falls are a natural for a day trip, and the bordering park offers camping and nature programs for a longer stay. Some mystery surrounds the origin of the name Bash-Bish, and folklore tells of an Indian maiden and her daughter who both died in these waters for love. Swirls of butterflies are said to mark their watery graves.

Farther north, in Columbia County, you'll find Hillsdale, a town well known to fans of American roots music, home to the annual music gatherings, the Falcon Ridge Festival every July and Winterhawk Bluegrass and Beyond Fest in August.

On the outskirts of town is Rodgers Book Barn, an antiquarian bookshop open since 1972. With more than 20,000 books for sale, the shop, which is an actual barn, is a soothing place to browse without pressure to buy. Ensconced by the musty scent of aged literature, a customer can meander down one of the many interwoven aisles stacked to the ceiling with publications. In a special spot labeled the Beneath Nook are free books and others that can be bought for up to 25 cents. The Book Barn's stock is haphazardly arranged in spots, so think of it as a treasure hunt.

As for treasures, I've left some I know of in these parts unmentioned and surely there are many waiting to be discovered. What you will certainly encounter on a Route 22 road trip, as I did recently with my cousin and years ago with my brothers, are roadways uncluttered with traffic, lined with cows and horses and peppered with roadside fresh fruit and vegetable stands. You'll hear a waiter in a diner cheerfully ask,

"You folks want coffee?" while being shown to a booth. You'll
see open space, perhaps an eagle in flight; smell fresh air and,
maybe, even hear yourself think.

Grandmother's Sunday Dinner
Patricia Hampl

Patricia Hampl (born in 1946) was raised in St. Paul, Minnesota,
and graduated from the University of Minnesota, where she currently teaches. She also spent time studying at the Iowa Writer's
Workshop. Hampl works primarily as an essayist, and her Czech
heritage remains a central theme in much of her writing.

My Thoughts in Writing

1. Trace Hampl's essay for the steps involved in the traditional
   process she describes. Which ones seem to be the most significant and why? Which ones reveal the type of person
   Hampl's grandmother was, the values she possessed?
2. Hampl uses specific and vivid sensory details to make you
   feel as though you are there having Sunday dinner with
   her family and her. How do these sensory details help her
   convey the point she is trying to make about her grandmother's Sunday dinners?
3. Hampl feels her grandmother is a virtuoso at serving dinner and that what she does is an art. What evidence does
   she provide to support her opinion of her grandmother
   and her grandmother's tradition? How does Hampl's retro-
   spective perspective affect her understanding of the value
   of her grandmother's Sunday dinners? What role did they
   play in her life and how did they serve her grandmother?

---- ✦ ----

Food was the potent center of my grandmother's life. Maybe
the immense amount of time it took to prepare meals during most of her life accounted for her passion. Or it may have

been her years of work in various kitchens on the hill and later, in the house of Justice Butler: after all, she was a professional. Much later, when she was dead and I went to Prague, I came to feel the motto I knew her by best—*Come eat*—was not, after all, a personal statement, but a racial one, the *cri de coeur* of Middle Europe.

Often, on Sundays, the entire family gathered for dinner at her house. Dinner was 1 P.M. My grandmother would have preferred the meal to be at the old time of noon, but her children had moved their own Sunday dinner hour to the more fashionable (it was felt) 4 o'clock, so she compromised. Sunday breakfast was something my mother liked to do in a big way, so we arrived at my grandmother's hardly out of the reverie of waffles and orange rolls, before we were propped like rag dolls in front of a pork roast and sauerkraut, dumplings, hot buttered carrots, rye bread and rollikey, pickles and olives, apple pie and ice cream. And coffee.

Coffee was a food in that house, not a drink. I always begged for some because the magical man on the Hills Brothers can with his turban and long robe scattered with stars and his gold slippers with pointed toes, looked deeply happy as he drank from his bowl. The bowl itself reminded me of soup, Campbell's chicken noodle soup, my favorite food. The distinct adultness of coffee and the robed man with his deep-drinking pleasure made it clear why the grownups lingered so long at the table. The uncles smoked cigars then, and the aunts said, "Oh, those cigars."

My grandmother, when she served dinner, was a virtuoso hanging on the edge of her own ecstatic performance. She seemed dissatisfied, almost querulous until she had corralled everybody into their chairs around the table, which she tried to do the minute they got into the house. No cocktails, no hors d'oeuvres (pronounced, by some of the family, "horse's ovaries"), just business. She was a little power crazed: she had us and, by God, we were going to eat. She went about it like a goose breeder forcing pellets down the gullets of those dumb birds.

5   She flew between her chair and the kitchen, always finding more this, extra that. She'd given you the *wrong* chicken breast the first time around; now she'd found the *right* one: eat

it too, eat it fast, because after the chicken comes the rhubarb pie. Rhubarb pie with a thick slice of cheddar cheese that it was imperative every single person eat.

We had to eat fast because something was always out there in the kitchen panting and charging the gate, champing at the bit, some mound of rice or a Jell-O fruit salad or vegetable casserole or pie was out there, waiting to be let loose into the dining room.

She had the usual trite routines: the wheedlings, the silent pout ("What! You don't like my brussels sprouts? I thought you liked *my* brussels sprouts," versus your wife's/ sister's/mother's. "I made that pie just for you," etc., etc.). But it was the way she tossed around the old clichés and the overused routines, mixing them up and dealing them out shamelessly, without irony, that made her a pro. She tended to peck at her own dinner. Her plate, piled with food, was a kind of stage prop, a mere bending to convention. She liked to eat, she was even a greedy little stuffer, but not on these occasions. She was a woman possessed by an idea, given over wholly to some phantasmagoria of food, a mirage of stuffing, a world where the endless chicken and the infinite lemon pie were united at last at the shore of the oceanic soup plate that her children and her children's children alone could drain . . . if only they would try.

She was there to bolster morale, to lead the troops, to give the sharp command should we falter on the way. The futility of saying no was supreme, and no one ever tried it. How could a son-in-law, already weakened near the point of imbecility by the once, twice, thrice charge to the barricades of pork and mashed potato, be expected to gather his feeble wit long enough to ignore the final call of his old commander when she sounded the alarm: "Pie, Fred?"

Just when it seemed as if the food-crazed world she had created was going to burst, that she had whipped and frothed us like a sack of boiled potatoes under her masher, just then she pulled it all together in one easeful stroke like the pro she was.

She stood in the kitchen doorway, her little round Napoleonic self sheathed in a cotton flowered pinafore apron, the table draped in its white lace cloth but spotted now with gravy and beet juice, the troops mumbling indistinctly as they waited at their posts for they knew not what. We looked up at her stupidly, weakly. She said nonchalantly, "Anyone want another piece of pie?" No, no more pie, somebody said. The rest of the rabble grunted along with him. She stood there with the coffeepot and laughed and said, "Good! Because there *isn't* any more pie."

No more pie. We'd eaten it all, we'd put away everything in that kitchen. We were exhausted and she, gambler hostess that she was (but it was her house she was playing), knew she could offer what didn't exist, knew us, knew what she'd wrought. There was a sense of her having won, won something. There were no divisions among us now, no adults, no children. Power left the second and third generations and returned to the source, the grandmother who reduced us to mutters by her art.

That wasn't the end of it. At 5 P.M. there was "lunch"— sandwiches and beer; the sandwiches were made from the leftovers (mysteriously renewable resources, those roasts). And at about 8 P.M. we were at the table again for coffee cake and coffee, the little man in his turban and his coffee ecstasy and his pointed shoes set on the kitchen table as my grandmother scooped out the coffee and dumped it into a big enamel pot with a crushed eggshell. By then everyone was alive and laughing again, the torpor gone. My grandfather had been inviting the men, one by one, into the kitchen during the afternoon where he silently (the austere version of memory—but he must have talked, must have said *something*) handed them jiggers of whiskey, and watched them put the shot down in one swallow. Then he handed them a beer, which they took out in the living room. I gathered that the *little* drink in the tiny glass shaped like a beer mug was some sort of antidote for the *big* drink of beer. He sat on the chair in the kitchen with a bottle of beer on the floor next to him and played his concertina, allowing society to form itself around him—while he lived he was the center—but not seeking it, not going into the living room. And not talking. He held to his music and the kindly, medicinal administration of whiskey.

By evening, it seemed we could eat endlessly, as if we'd had some successful inoculation at dinner and could handle anything. I stayed in the kitchen after they all reformed in the dining room at the table for coffee cake. I could hear them, but the little man in his starry yellow robe was on the table in the kitchen and I put my head down on the oil cloth very near the curled and delighted tips of his pointed shoes, and I slept. Whatever laughter there was, there was. But something sweet and starry was in the kitchen and I lay down beside it, my stomach full, warm, so safe I'll live the rest of my life off the fat of that vast family security.

Waking Up the Rake
Linda Hogan

Born in 1947, Linda Hogan has worked a variety of jobs over the years. The following essay chronicles a portion of her experience as a volunteer at the Minnesota Wildlife Rehabilitation Clinic. She is now a teacher, poet, writer, and screenwriter whose works include a collection of poems, a collection of short stories, and a novel.

My Thoughts in Writing

1. How does the rake, like the earth it touches, become a living thing through Hogan's discussion of it? How does raking itself become an art?
2. The work Hogan does is repetitive, but meaningful. What does she tell us is the value and purpose of such repetitive work? What are the rewards she finds in it?
3. A process is usually learned through a set of fairly detailed instructions, whether written or verbal. How does Hogan describe the process of raking without giving us step-by-step instructions? What is the purpose of Hogan's discussion of the process of raking? How does the

process serve Hogan herself? In what ways does this traditional and ritualistic work relate to life and life processes?

———————— ✦ ————————

In the still dark mornings, my grandmother would rise up from her bed and put wood in the stove. When the fire began to burn, she would sit in front of its warmth and let down her hair. It had never been cut and it knotted down in two long braids. When I was fortunate enough to be there, in those red Oklahoma mornings, I would wake up with her, stand behind her chair, and pull the brush through the long strands of her hair. It cascaded down her back, down over the chair, and touched the floor.

We were the old and the new, bound together in front of the snapping fire, woven like a lifetime's tangled growth of hair. I saw my future in her body and face, and her past was alive in me. We were morning people, and in all of earth's mornings the new intertwines with the old. Even new, a day itself is ancient, old with earth's habit of turning over and over again.

Years later, I was sick, and I went to a traditional healer. The healer was dark and thin and radiant. The first night I was there, she also lit a fire. We sat before it, smelling the juniper smoke. She asked me to tell her everything, my life spoken in words, a case history of living, with its dreams and losses, the scars and wounds we all bear from being in the world. She smoked me with cedar smoke, wrapped a sheet around me, and put me to bed, gently, like a mother caring for her child.

The next morning she nudged me awake and took me outside to pray. We faced east where the sun was beginning its journey on our side of earth.

10   The following morning in red dawn, we went outside and prayed. The sun was a full orange eye rising up the air. The morning after that we did the same, and on Sunday we did likewise.

The next time I visited her it was a year later, and again we went through the same prayers, standing outside facing the early sun. On the last morning I was there, she left for her job in town. Before leaving, she said, "Our work is our altar."

Those words have remained with me.

Now I am a disciple of birds. The birds that I mean are eagles, owls, and hawks. I clean cages at the Birds of Prey Rehabilitation Foundation. It is the work I wanted to do, in order to spend time inside the gentle presence of the birds.

There is a Sufi saying that goes something like this: "Yes, worship God, go to church, sing praises, but first tie your camel to the post." This cleaning is the work of tying the camel to a post.

I pick up the carcasses and skin of rats, mice, and of rabbits. Some of them have been turned inside out by the sharp-beaked eaters, so that the leathery flesh becomes a delicately veined coat for the inner fur. It is a boneyard. I rake the smooth fragments of bones. Sometimes there is a leg or shank of deer to be picked up.

In this boneyard, the still-red vertebrae lie on the ground beside an open rib cage. The remains of a rabbit, a small intestinal casing, holds excrement like beads in a necklace. And there are the clean, oval pellets the birds spit out, filled with fur, bone fragments and now and then, a delicate sharp claw that looks as if it were woven inside. A feather, light and soft, floats down a current of air, and it is also picked up.

Over time, the narrow human perspective from which we view things expands. A deer carcass begins to look beautiful and rich in its torn redness, the muscle and bone exposed in the shape life took on for a while as it walked through meadows and drank at creeks.

And the bone fragments have their own stark beauty, the clean white jaw bones with ivory teeth small as the head of a pin still in them. I think of medieval physicians trying to learn about our private, hidden bodies by cutting open the stolen dead and finding the splendor inside, the grace of every red organ, and the smooth, gleaming bone.

This work is an apprenticeship, and the birds are the teachers. Sweet-eyed barn owls, such taskmasters, asking us to be still and slow and to move in time with their rhythms, not our own. The short-eared owls with their startling yellow eyes require the full presence of a human. The marsh hawks, behind their branches, watch our every move.

There is a silence needed here before a person enters the bordered world the birds inhabit, so we stop and compose ourselves before entering their doors, and we listen to the musical calls of the eagles, the sound of wings in air, the way their feet with sharp claws, many larger than our own hands, grab hold of a perch. Then we know we are ready to enter, and they are ready for us.

The most difficult task the birds demand is that we learn to be equal to them, to feel our way into an intelligence that is different from our own. A friend, awed at the thought of working with eagles, said, "Imagine knowing an eagle." I answered her honestly, "It isn't so much that we know the eagles. It's that they know us."

And they know that we are apart from them, that as humans we have somehow fallen from our animal grace, and because of that we maintain a distance from them, though it is not always a distance of heart. The places we inhabit, even sharing a common earth, must remain distinct and separate. It was our presence that brought most of them here in the first place, nearly all of them injured in a clash with the human world. They have been shot, or hit by cars, trapped in leg hold traps, poisoned, ensnared in wire fences. To ensure their survival, they must remember us as the enemies that we are. We are the embodiment of a paradox; we are the wounders and we are the healers.

There are human lessons to be learned here, in the work. Fritjof Capra wrote: "Doing work that has to be done over and over again helps us to recognize the natural cycles of growth and decay, of birth and death, and thus become aware of the dynamic order of the universe." And it is true, in whatever we do, the brushing of hair, the cleaning of cages, we begin to see the larger order of things. In this place, there is a constant coming to terms with both the sacred place life occupies, and with death. Like one of those early physicians who discovered the strange, inner secrets of our human bodies, I'm filled with awe at the very presence of life, not just the birds, but a horse contained in its living fur, a dog alive and running. What a marvel it is, the fine shape life takes in all of us. It is equally marvelous that life is quickly turned back to the earth-colored ants and the soft white maggots that are time's best and closest companions. To sit with the eagles and their flutelike songs, listening to the longer flute of wind sweep through the lush grasslands, is to begin to know the natural laws that exist apart from our own written ones.

One of those laws, that we carry deep inside us, is intuition. It is lodged in a place even the grave-robbing doctors could not discover. It's a blood-written code that directs us through life. The founder of this healing center, Sigrid Ueblacker, depends on this inner knowing. She watches, listens, and feels her way to an understanding of each eagle and owl. This vision, as I call it, directs her own daily work at healing the injured birds and returning them to the wild.

"Sweep the snow away," she tells me. "The Swainson's hawks should be in Argentina this time of year and should not have to stand in the snow."   20

I sweep.

And that is in the winter when the hands ache from the cold, and the water freezes solid and has to be broken out for the birds, fresh buckets carried over icy earth from the well. In summer, it's another story. After only a few hours the food begins to move again, as if resurrected to life. A rabbit shifts a bit. A mouse turns. You could say that they have been resurrected, only with a life other than the one that left them. The moving skin swarms with flies and their offspring, ants, and a few wasps, busy at their own daily labor.

Even aside from the expected rewards for this work, such as seeing an eagle healed and winging across the sky it fell from, there are others. An occasional snake, beautiful and sleek, finds its way into the cage one day, eats a mouse and is too fat to leave, so we watch its long muscular life stretched out in the tall grasses. Or, another summer day, taking branches to be burned with a pile of wood near the little creek, a large turtle with a dark and shining shell slips soundlessly into the water, its presence a reminder of all the lives beyond these that occupy us.

One green morning, an orphaned owl perches nervously above me while I clean. Its downy feathers are roughed out. It appears to be twice its size as it clacks its beak at me, warning me: stay back. Then, fearing me the way we want it to, it bolts off the perch and flies, landing by accident onto the wooden end of my rake, before it sees that a human is an extension of the tool, and it flies again to a safer place, while I return to raking.

25   The word "rake" means to gather or heap up, to smooth
the broken ground. And that's what this work is, all of it, the
smoothing over of broken ground, the healing of the severed
trust we humans hold with earth. We gather it back together
again with great care, take the broken pieces and fragments
and return them to the sky. It is work at the borderland between species, at the boundary between injury and healing.

There is an art to raking, a very fine art, one with rhythm in
it, and life. On the days I do it well, the rake wakes up. Wood
that came from dark dense forests seems to return to life. The
water that rose up through the rings of that wood, the minerals
of earth mined upward by the burrowing tree roots, all come
alive. My own fragile hand touches the wood, a hand full of my
own life, including that which rose each morning early to watch
the sun return from the other side of the planet, Over time, these
hands will smooth the rake's wooden handle down to a sheen.

Raking. It is a labor round and complete, smooth and new
as an egg, and the rounding seasons of the world revolving in
time and space. All things, even our own heartbeats and sweat,
are in it, part of it. And that work, that watching the turning
over of life, becomes a road into what is essential. Work is the
country of hands, and they want to live there in the dailiness of
it, the repetition that is time's language of prayer, a common
tongue. Everything is there, in that language, in the humblest of
labor. The rake wakes up and the healing is in it. The shadows
of leaves that once fell beneath the tree the handle came from
are in that labor, and the rabbits that passed this way, on the altar of our work. And when the rake wakes up, all earth's gods
are reborn and they dance and sing in the dusty air around us.

Saturday Afternoon, When Chores Are Done

HARRYETTE MULLEN

Born in 1952, Harryette Mullen is the author of four books of
poetry and currently teaches African-American literature and

Creative Writing at the University of California at Los Angeles. Her work can be found in many anthologies including *Trouble the Water* and *Gertrude Stein Awards for Innovative American Poetry and African-American Literature* edited by Al Young and Ishmael Reed.

My Thoughts in Writing

1. The first two lines of the poem describe the setting surrounding the process engaged in as the poem progresses. Why is it important that we understand the setting? How is this setting related to the process described in the poem?

2. When the speaker was young, her mother told her that plaiting hair "just takes practice." Why did her mother say this? To what other thing(s) do the mother's words refer? How do you know?

3. How does the process of plaiting hair serve the speaker? What is its primary purpose? Why is it important to the speaker that her daughters learn this process as well?

———————— ✦ ————————

I've cleaned house
and the kitchen smells like pine.
I can hear the kids yelling
through the back screen door.
While they play tug-of-war   5
with an old jumprope
and while these blackeyed peas
boil on the stove,
I'm gonna sit here at the table
and plait my hair.   10

I oil my hair and brush it soft.
Then, with the brush in my lap,
I gather the hair in my hands,
pull the strands smooth and tight,
and weave three sections into a fat shiny braid   15
that hangs straight down my back.

I remember mama teaching me to plait my hair
one Saturday afternoon when chores were done.

My fingers were stubby and short.
I could barely hold three strands at once,   20
and my braids would fray apart
no sooner than I'd finished them.
Mama said, "Just takes practice, is all."
Now my hands work swiftly, doing easy
what was once so hard to do.   25

Between time on the job,
keeping house, and raising two girls by myself,
there's never much time like this,
for thinking and being alone.
Time to gather life together   30
before it unravels like an old jumprope
and comes apart at the ends.

Suddenly I notice the silence.
The noisy tug-of-war has stopped.
I get up to check out back,   35
see what my girls are up to now.
I look out over the kitchen sink,
where the sweet potato plant
spreads green in the window.
They sit quietly on the back porch steps,   40
Melinda plaiting Carla's hair
into a crooked braid.

Older daughter,
you are learning what I am learning:
to gather the strands together   45
with strong fingers,
to keep what we do
from coming apart at the ends.

Impressions of an Indian Childhood
Zitkala-Sa

Born in 1876, on a reservation in South Dakota, Zitkala-Sa
was the first American Indian woman to write her story with-

out aid of an editor, interpreter, or ethnographer. Her works reflect not only her concern for the rights of Native Americans, but her struggle to overcome assimilation and celebrate cultural heritage.

My Thoughts in Writing

1. Zitkala-Sa writes that she "loved best the evening meal." What about the evening meal makes it so special? Who is involved and what are their roles?
2. What is the process Zitkala-Sa introduces us to in her piece? What are the steps of this process and how important is each one to the product itself?
3. It is obvious that Zitkala-Sa enjoys the traditional process in which she engages. What purpose does it serve Zitkala-Sa as an individual and how does it serve the members of her community?

———————— ✦ ————————

I loved best the evening meal, for that was the time old legends were told. I was always glad when the sun hung low in the west, for then my mother sent me to invite the neighboring old men and women to eat supper with us. Running all the way to the wigwams, I halted shyly at the entrances. . . . It was not any fear that made me so dumb when out upon such a happy errand; nor was it that I wished to withhold the invitation, for it was all I could do to observe this very proper silence. But it was a sensing of the atmosphere, to assure myself that I should not hinder other plans. . . . The old folks knew the meaning of my pauses. . . .

At the arrival of our guests I sat close to my mother, and did not leave her side without first asking her consent. I ate my supper in quiet, listening patiently to the talk of the old people, wishing all the time that they would begin the stories I loved best. At last, when I could not wait any longer, I whispered in mother's ear, "Ask them to tell an Iktomi story, mother." Soothing my impatience, my mother said aloud, "My little daughter is anxious to hear your legends."

As each in turn began to tell a legend, I pillowed my head in my mother's lap; and lying flat upon my back, I watched the stars as they peeped down upon me, one by one.

Sample Student Essay

My Family Tradition

MELISSA CRANER

One of many traditions my family and I take part in is picking out our Christmas tree and decorating it. It seems to be a long drawn out process, but in the end it brings nothing but joy to my mom, my step-dad, and me. No matter how busy our lives get, this is one tradition we always follow.

This event takes place long before Christmas. It takes place the weekend after Thanksgiving. My mom, my step-dad, and I will venture out to a tree farm to find that perfect Christmas tree. When we arrive at the tree farm, we head toward the tractor that has a cart attached to it. The cart is filled with bales of hay for us to sit on. When everyone is situated, the tractor starts up and begins to pull us to the endless number of trees to pick from. When we get close to our destination, the tractor slows to a complete stop and we exit through the back. As we exit through the back, we brush the hay off of our clothes. We enter the long aisles of Christmas trees and begin searching for the one we will all agree on. Finally, after hours of looking, we have our tree tagged, cut down, and wrapped for us to take home.

As my step-dad brings the Christmas tree into the house, my mother hurries into the family room to make room for it. I help my mom by moving the coffee table closer to the fireplace. My step-dad sets up the tree in the stand while my mom sits on the couch waiting patiently, hoping he will have it standing in the right direction when he is finished—which means it will be standing with its bare spots facing the back. When my mom approves of the tree's positioning, my step-dad then fills the stand with water. At this point, it is usually too late to start decorating the tree, so I help my mom clean up the pine needles the tree left behind. Then we call it a night.

The next evening, we gather in the family room and prepare for the decorating of the Christmas tree. My mom and I sit on the couch and unwrap the burgundy velvet bows and shiny Christmas ornaments. We sort through them, searching for those that have been broken from being packed away in the attic over the summer months. After untangling the Christmas lights, my step-dad plugs them in to see which lights he will have to replace. Having replaced any bulbs, he then carefully strings each strand of lights onto a branch of the tree.

When he is done, my mother will inspect the lights, making sure there are no noticeable gaps in between each strand of lights.

My mother then starts decorating the tree by placing the velvet bows on the tip of almost each branch. Just about every five minutes she stops to stand back and see how the tree looks. Almost every time she stops, she will turn to me and say, "Well, how does it look so far?" Of course, I always answer: "It looks great, Mom!" When she is done putting the bows on the tree, I start to hang the ornaments on the branches. As it starts to get later into the night, I put the last ornament onto the tree and once again we call it a night.

The second evening of decorating begins as we meet again in the family room. Having the Christmas tree almost finished, we only have three more things to do. To give the tree a snowy effect, my mom and I each take a can of fake snow and spray the undecorated parts of the tree. When we are done spraying the tree, my step-dad lays a tree skirt around the bottom. To put the finishing touch on the Christmas tree, one of us gets on a ladder to place an angel at the very top. When all is finished, we sit on the couch together and admire what our hard work has just created.

As our lives seem to be getting busier, we don't get to spend as much time with each other as we would like. I now truly look forward to that hay ride we take as a family to pick out the Christmas tree. I also appreciate the days it takes to decorate that carefully chosen tree. For it is not just time spent decorating a tree, it is time spent together as a family.

My Thoughts in Writing

1. What is Craner's main point in writing about her family's tradition? Find the sentence or sentences in which she states her main point. How does she view this family tradition? How do you know?
2. What are the steps involved in the Craner Christmas-tree-picking tradition? How involved in the process of this tradition are the members of Craner's family? How important is each member's involvement?
3. Find the places in Craner's essay where she uses vivid sensory detail. What is the effect on you as a reader of such fine detailing and such attention to each particular step of the process she is describing? How important is it that you understand each step of the process? Explain your answer.

The Readings Come Together

1. In the introduction to this chapter, three general categories of process-related traditions were identified. Into which one(s) would you place the traditions that Hample and Hogan describe? What are the similarities in the processes Hampl and Hogan describe? How are they different?

2. Both Hampl and Zitkala-Sa describe the work of their elders. Hampl describes what her grandmother does and Zitkala-Sa describes what the older tribal members do. What is similar about the way Hampl and Zitkala-Sa describe the work done by their elders? How are Hampl and Zitkala-Sa similarly affected by the folklore processes they witness?

3. Hampl describes her grandmother's cooking as an art, and Hogan describes raking in the same manner. How do the authors justify their use of the term *art* in reference to the subjects of their essays? How are cooking and raking similar in this regard?

4. In terms of purpose, how is the process Craner describes similar to the processes described by Zitkala-Sa and Polese?

5. What role in the process of tradition do the elders play in the selections by written, Hampl, Hogan, Craner, and Zitkala-Sa? When the selections are brought together, what general theme about elders is conveyed?

6. At the close of Polese's essay, she tells us that her tradition—time on the road—offers a view of open space and eagles in flight, the smell of open air, and time to connect with her inner thoughts. The traditions described in the other essays also offer time for reflection. Using the essays to illustrate your point, explain why time for reflection is so important and how the traditions make this time possible.

There's Something More out There

Part I

At-Home Activity:

This activity may require interviewing. In your journal, create a list of the people within your family or community who engage in process-oriented traditions, such as cleaning, gardening, baking, quilting, sewing, craft making, or woodworking. Or focus on one family or community member who has made a task of a much-loved and necessary ritual (such as Hogan does with raking). When you have your list compiled, consider how the process-oriented traditions or rituals serve the individuals who engage in them. How do they convey family, community, or personal values?

Part II

Classroom Storytelling Session

Sharing traditions/rituals of family and community members, figuring the how and why. In groups of three or four, share the discoveries you made while completing the exercise above. Discuss how family and community members use process-oriented traditions/rituals and the purposes those traditions serve.

Part III

Journal Entry

Option 1.   Outline the steps involved in one tradition specific to your family or community (a meal gathering, a birthday, a holiday, a vacation, etc.).

Option 2.   Identify and describe a process-oriented tradition a family or community member engages in, such as woodworking, quilting, or baking.

Part IV

Writing Assignment

Using one or more of the readings and one of your journal entries, create an essay that focuses on the significance of a tradition's process—be it a celebration, hobby, or personal task. Relate what you believe is the meaning of the traditional process described in the reading(s) to the traditional process you intend to focus on in your own writing. Your essay should convey the meaning of a tradition/ritual process to you, your family or community, or to the person who engages in it. To help you in writing about the tradition, you might interview family or community members. For instance, if your grandmother loves baking (as mine does), ask her about her favorite family recipes—those that have been handed down from one generation to the next. Choose one to record. Find out as much as you can about the recipe: where it originated, whether it is or was prepared for certain holidays, what other foods are traditionally served with it. The focus of your essay could be the significance of the dish itself to the cook who made or makes it. Or the focus of your essay could be the significance of the act of engaging in the tradition to the person involved. For instance, as I learned from my grandmother, *making* her famous coconut cake—the preparation and the steps involved—is my grandmother's way of paying tribute to the days she spent baking with her own mother and grandmother.

Traditions: A Changing Same

THE FOLKLORE FOCUS

Family and Community Traditions: The Familiar Meets the Unfamiliar

Fairly early in life, most of us learn that change is inevitable. Truth be told, there is very little about our lives that will remain the same as the years go by. Perhaps this is why we hold fast to our traditions, for they give us a sense of the familiar; they make us feel as though there is something in life that we can count on to remain pretty much the same. Our lives may be drastically altered by time and circumstance, but we like to believe our traditions are steadfast, loyal to the way things were. However, the fact is that just as change is necessary in our lives in general, so, too, is it necessary when it comes to our traditions. Why? Because our traditions would not remain vital or useful if they were not altered according to the modifications made in the lives of individuals and communities. Contrary to popular belief, our traditions are not preserved through strict adherence to the way things have always been done. Rather, they are maintained through careful attention to the changing needs of those who engage in them. In a way, a tradition is a kind of changing same; there is room for alterations, given the way our lives shift and the differences in individuals and communities, yet there is also something that remains constant. Think about the essay "Meaning of hunt lost from afar" by Nicole Brodeur in Chapter 4. Although the Makah tribe's whale hunt tradition had been transformed by time and forces beyond their control, the members of the tribe accepted the changes because they agreed that the essence of the tradition is what mattered. If the tradition, altered as it was, continued to bring the tribe together, providing them a link to the past, and renewing their sense of community, then the tribe could manage the uncontrollable, unforeseen, or deliberate alterations to the tradition.

This does not mean that we won't feel sad when the pattern of a tradition changes. Most of us do. But your work in the previous chapters illustrates that a tradition's value is more than a matter of its shape. That is, while you may look forward to your family's Sunday dinner at Grandma's house, it's probably not the specifics of the routine of the day that matter the most. Chances are that what is most important is what the tradition does for your family—it brings all of you together and renews your ties to each other. The changing nature of our traditions reflects the changing nature of our lives. And while all this change can be a scary thing, if the alterations to our traditions are handled with care, they should not detract from what we look to our traditions for: stability, security, structure, a sense of who we are and where we belong.

This chapter centers on the relationship between past and present traditions and the variations in like traditions among differing groups. You will be encouraged to study the way traditions change over time and are uniquely shaped depending on the needs of those engaging in them. The readings selected for this chapter and the questions that follow them will help you do this. As a whole, the selections illustrate not only the way traditions change, but the effects of those changes on individuals and groups. The questions that precede each selection require you to further analyze the readings, to examine the role of change in the life of traditions, and to think carefully about what is said regarding the changing nature of traditions. Consider the way the writers use tone, narration, dialogue, and sensory detail to convey and to trace the changing shape of their traditions and to reflect their feelings regarding the same. Through your careful analysis of these selections and the changing traditions they present, you will prepare yourself for writing about the way the traditions in your life have shifted over the years. In addition, your journal entries, class discussions, and outside research will prepare you for writing about what you have in common with and what you can learn from the traditions of others.

Carnival in Rio Is Dancing to More Commercial Beat

Larry Rohter

As the Central American correspondent for *Newsweek* magazine (1980–1982) and *The New York Times* (1994–1981), Larry Rohter has written extensively on international affairs. He is now *The New York Times'* bureau chief in Rio de Janeiro.

My Thoughts in Writing

1. According to Rohter, Carnival has changed quite a bit over the years. Trace the essay for the changes he describes and compare Carnival today to what it once was. Which Carnival would Rohter choose? Why? How can you tell? Use specific words and phrases from the essay to illustrate your answer.

2. If it is actually "natural for any form of folk culture to evolve and change" what, according to Fernando Pamplona, is wrong with the changes to the Carnival? What evidence does Rohter provide to back up Pamplona's assertions?

3. How has the general public reacted to Carnival's changes? What is happening to Carnival as a result? Use specific selections from the text to illustrate your point.

--- ◆ ---

Picking the King of Carnival here used to be easy: Find the city's fattest, jolliest man and stick a crown on his head. But after being reproached for weighing in at nearly 500 pounds, the current Rei Momo has succumbed to critics, begun exercising, changed his diet and lost 175 pounds over the last four years.

To connoisseurs of Carnival, the heretical emergence of a "Rei Momo light" is one of the many indignities recently inflicted on the spectacle that natives of Rio once regarded as an expression of the character and creativity of their city. As they see it, the annual Bacchanalia, which begins this weekend, is becoming less a people's festival than a tightly controlled industry.

"It's natural for any form of folk culture to evolve and change, but the official Carnival parade is turning into a pasteurized product, confined to a cold environment in which the creators of the samba no longer make the rules," said Fernando Pamplona, a renowned choreographer and judge of the Carnival competition. "We live in a capitalist society, so even something like folklore is subject to massification and commercialization."

As always, the focal point of the five-day celebration this year will be the Carnival parade, with its scantily clad dancers, pounding drums and elaborate floats. Over two nights, 14 associations, known as "samba schools," will compete in hopes of putting on the most dazzling show and winning the championship that will give them bragging rights for the next year.

5   But in place of knowledgeable samba fans, the stands along the parade route are increasingly filled with tourists, celebrities and high rollers, many of whom are guests of corporations that have spent huge sums on luxury boxes. And instead of choosing parade themes developed by their members and based on folk or mythological subjects, many samba schools now are paid by large companies to choose topics that are thinly disguised commercials. Outsiders are even infiltrating the parade, to the point that a majority of those parading with sections of some samba schools are not even members. Tourists as far away as Japan or Scandinavia can now buy package tours that include the right to parade with a samba school, wearing a tailored costume at a cost of an additional $300 or so.

"Those people can't sing, they can't dance, and they don't even bother to learn the lyrics to the theme song of the samba school they are parading with," said Dulce Tupi, a scholar who has written on the history of Carnival and served on the official parade jury. "All they do is detract from the beauty of the show and damage the performance of the samba school."

Traditionally, the lavish Carnival costumes and floats were put together by seamstresses and carpenters from the neighborhoods around a samba school. But those functions are largely subcontracted to professional companies now: Last year, one school had points deducted because its costumes arrived so late that dancers were unable to start their procession on time.

"In the old days, the samba school supporters lived close to where they worked and had time to participate in the life of the school," said Joãosinho Trinta, an acclaimed samba school director. "Now they get up at four in the morning for a three-hour commute to work, and by the time they finally get back home, tired and hungry, all they want to do is sit in the living room and watch television."

Criminal gangs are now in control of most hillside slums where the samba schools were born, and that has also had an effect. Though the schools have been largely successful in keeping drugs out of their popular weekly rehearsals, waves of killings and robberies have forced several to move those performances into middle-class areas. The relocations attract tourists but make it more difficult and costly for their traditional supporters to take part.

Unable to attend the parade, whose tickets are increasingly priced out of their reach and quickly bought by travel agencies, many samba fans are reduced to watching on television. But what they are seeing is a shift away from the samba, which has been sped up to meet the time requirements imposed by networks, to a spectacle that emphasizes the visual over the musical.

10

A decade ago, the record containing that year's theme sambas of the 14 competing clubs could be expected to sell as many as two million copies. Now the same record is lucky to reach one-tenth that number.

In addition, television has encouraged scores of models and actresses to use the Carnival parade to promote their careers. Many of those B-level or would-be stars are affiliated with the network broadcasting the show or have undergone plastic surgery or breast implants specifically to parade naked in front of 70,000 people at the Sambadrome here and the millions watching in Brazil and abroad.

"People who really love Carnival want to hear the samba sung, see how the dancers are dancing and get a really good look at the floats and decorations," said Antônio Carlos Seiblitz, a 49-year-old lawyer here. "Instead, what we get are endless interviews with celebrities who have no genuine connection with Carnival, punctuated by occasional glimpses of the real thing."

But Carnival consists of much more than the official parade, and as the populace grows more alienated from that event, other forms of celebration are benefiting. Masked balls are proliferating and are more popular than ever, and the informal neighborhood associations known as blocos or bandas, considered moribund just a couple of decades ago, are making a remarkable comeback.

15   All around the city, local groups with whimsical or irreverent names like Christ's Armpit, Leopard's Breath, Meeting Without a Parade, Affinity Is Almost Love, and Hang On So You Don't Fall Down have already taken to the streets, encouraging residents to dress up and join them. According to a recent study, the number of such groups has doubled in less than a decade, and popular participation in them is zooming.

"With the parade having become an event just for the elite and tickets so expensive, my energy now goes into the neighborhood celebrations," said Isabel Cristina Lopes, 34, a marketing executive who used to parade with the Beija-Flor samba school. "You need to be an important person to get into the parade, but with the blocos, everyone can participate."

Others in search of the true Carnival spirit are abandoning Rio altogether in favor of cities like Recife and Salvador. There, traditional musical forms associated with Carnival, like the frevo and maracatu in Recife and the ear-splitting electric trios that play atop trucks cruising the streets of Salvador, have largely pushed aside Rio's commercialized samba as favorites.

"There is a tendency to try to centralize and domesticate Carnival, but it seems not to be working completely," said Roberto da Matta, a Brazilian anthropologist who has written extensively on the festival and teaches at the University of Notre Dame. "Carnival refuses to be dominated by one form or style, by one parade or event, and is coming to life again outside those ordained centers as old forms reappear and are reconstructed."

Preparations for Seder
Michael S. Glaser

Michael S. Glaser has taught literature and creative writing at St. Mary's College in Maryland and has served as a poet-in-the-schools with the Maryland State Arts Council. He served as editor of *The Cooke Book: A Seasoning of Poets*, (1996) and he has written numerous collections of poetry.

My Thoughts in Writing

1. In the poem, the speaker mentions the way things have changed since his grandmother made schmaltz and crackling. How does his engagement in the tradition differ from his grandmother's? Is the change for the better or for the worse? Why? How would his father react to the change? Why do you think he conveys his father's reaction?
2. In terms of the meaning of the tradition, how important are the changes to it? How do you know? Explain your answer using specific words, lines, or phrases from the poem.
3. In the last stanza of the poem, the speaker compares the matzoh balls to freedom. What words does he use to make this comparison? How appropriate are they? And, finally, what does the tradition mean to the speaker? What does his engagement in it call to mind?

———————— ✦ ————————

Preparing schmaltz for matzoh balls,
I peel the skin off chickens, scrape yellow fat
from pink meat, think of my father: how he stood
at the elbow of his mother, eating the "cracklings"
she'd hand down from the stove, morsels of meat   5
fried free of the fat, as she rendered schmaltz
years ago, in Boston.

Today, preparing for Seder, I think of Grandmother
as I salvage these tasty cracklings, relish them
for myself, hand them to my children as I cut more   10
and more fat from the chicken: how much harder
for her, hot before the wood stove, peeling bits
of fat from the muscle of chickens that ran
free in the yard.

Now the fat is plentiful, preserved with chemicals.   15
The echo of my father's voice calls out warnings
of carcinogens in the fat of animals and I wonder
what I am doing to myself, my children. But this
is the eve of Passover. I am making matzoh balls.
My knife plunges under the skin for more fat.   20
I will not forsake the traditions of my ancestors.

At the Seder meal, we sip the chicken broth,
then cut into the matzoh balls, savory
with marrow and garlic, parsley and schmaltz,
remembering forty years in the desert, the freedom   25
of the promised land, succulent and dangerous,
bobbing before us like these matzoh balls we relish
and eat and praise the taste of, wanting more.

On Holidays and How to Make Them Work

Nikki Giovanni

Born in 1943 in Knoxville, Tennessee, Nikki Giovanni was
raised in Cincinnati, Ohio. As a student at Fisk University, she
was a member of the Writer's Workshop and the Student Non-
violent Coordinating Committee. Her continued interest in
writing and politics are reflected in her poetry and essays. Giovanni has been named Woman of the Year by *Ebony* magazine, and she currently teaches English at Virginia Polytechnic
Institute.

My Thoughts in Writing

1. Why does Giovanni take exception to the ways holidays are celebrated in America? What are Americans doing wrong? According to Giovanni, what are some of the holidays Americans celebrate inappropriately?

2. Although Giovanni is obviously displeased with the way Americans celebrate holidays, she mentions some of the benefits that come from our behavior. What are some of the benefits she lists? Is she serious about these benefits? How do you know? Use the text to prove your point.

3. What is Giovanni's main point about American holidays? Do you agree or disagree? Why? What might be the advantage in Americans celebrating holidays in the way they were intended to be celebrated—as "time of reflection on great men, great deeds, great people. Things like that." Have you ever celebrated one of the holidays she mentions in the way she describes? What was the effect?

———————— ✦ ————————

A proper holiday, coming from the medieval "holy day," is supposed to be a time of reflection on great men, great deeds, great people. Things like that. Somehow in America this didn't quite catch on. Take Labor Day. On Labor Day you take the day off, then go to the Labor Day sales and spend your devalued money with a clerk who is working. And organized labor doesn't understand why it suffers declining membership? Pshaw. Who wants to join an organization that makes you work on the day it designates as a day off? Plus, no matter how hidden the agenda, who wants a day off if they make you march in a parade and listen to some politicians talk on and on about nothing.

Hey. I'm a laborer. I used to work in Walgreen's on Linn Street. We were open every holiday and I, being among the junior people, always "got" to work the time-and-a-half holidays. I hated those people who came in. Every fool in the Western world, and probably in this universe, knows that Christmas is December 25. Has been that way for over a thousand years, yet there they'd be, standing outside the door, cold, bleary-eyed, waiting for us to open so they could purchase a present. Memorial Day, which used to be Armistice Day until we got into this situation of continuous war, was the official start of summer. We would want to be out with our boyfriends barbecuing . . . or something, but there we were behind the counter waiting to see who forgot that in order to barbecue you need: (1) a grill, (2) charcoal, (3) charcoal starter. My heart goes out to the twenty-four-hour grocery people, who are probably selling meat!

But hey. It's the American way. The big Fourth of July sales probably reduced the number of fatal injuries as people spent the entire day sober in malls, fighting over markdowns. Minor cuts and bruises were way up, though, I'll bet. And forget the great nonholiday, Presidents' Day. The damned thing could at least have a real name. What does that mean—Presidents' Day? Mostly that we don't care enough to take the time to say to Washington and Lincoln: Well done. But for sure, as a Black American I've got to go for it. Martin Luther King, Jr.'s birthday has come up for the first time as a national holiday. If we are serious about celebrating it, Steinberg's will be our first indication: GHETTO BLASTERS 30% OFF! FREE TAPE OF "I HAVE A DREAM" WITH EVERY VCR PURCHASED AT THE ALL-NEW GIGANTIC MARTY'S BIRTHDAY SALE. Then Wendy's will, just maybe, for Black patrons (and their liberal sympathizers) Burn-A-Burger to celebrate the special day. Procter & Gamble will withhold Clorox for the day, respectfully requesting that those Black spots be examined for their liberating influence. But what we really want, where we can know we have succeeded, is that every Federated department store offers 50 percent off to every colored patron who can prove he or she is Black in recognition of the days when colored citizens who were Black were not accorded all the privileges of other shoppers. That will be a big help because everybody will want to be Black for a Day. Sun tanneries will make fortunes during the week preceding MLK Day. Wig salons will reap great benefits. Dentists will have to hire extra help to put that distinctive gap between the middle front teeth. MLK Day will be accepted. And isn't that the heart of the American dream?

I really love a good holiday—it takes the people off the streets and puts them safely in the shopping malls. Now think about it. Aren't you proud to be with Uncle Sam?

All I Want

Luci Tapahonso

A Navajo Indian born in Shiprock, New Mexico, Luci Tapahonso strives to create works that reflect and comment upon her native heritage. She is an accomplished poet and has taught at the University of Mexico, Albuquerque.

My Thoughts in Writing

1. Tapahonso's poem is about the tradition of baking bread. From whom is the speaker learning a lesson about baking bread? What is the lesson? How do you know? Use the poem to explain your answer.
2. What is it about the tradition that the baker believes young people don't understand? How might the younger generation do things differently when it comes to baking bread?
3. What is the relevance of the son outside chopping wood? Why does the speaker turn our attention to him? What aspect of the tradition of baking bread might his presence highlight and reflect?

――――――― ✦ ―――――――

All I want is the bread to turn out like hers just once
          brown crust
          soft, airy insides
          rich and round
that is all.   5
So I ask her: How many cups?
          Ah yaa ah, she says,
          tossing flour and salt into a large, silver bowl.
          I don't measure with cups.

I just know by my hands,   10
just a little like this is right, see?
You young people always ask
those kinds of questions,
she says,
thrusting her arms into the dough   15
and turning it over and over again.
The table trembles with her movements.
I watch silently and this coffee is good,
                                    strong and fresh.
Outside, her son is chopping wood,   20
his body an intense arc.
The dull rhythm of winter
is the swinging of the axe
and the noise of children squeezing in
with the small sighs of wind   25
through the edges of the windows.

She pats and tosses it furiously
shaping balls of warm, soft dough.
There, we'll let it rise,
she says, sitting down now.   30
We drink coffee and there is nothing
like the warm smell of bread rising
on windy, woodchopping afternoons.

Black Music in Our Hands

BERNICE REAGON

Bernice Reagon grew up in Albany, Georgia, and attended Albany State College and Spelman College prior to earning her doctorate from Howard University in 1975. Her university studies focused on black history and music, and her work since then has done the same. Her writing reflects the importance of the work she has done as director of the Washington, D.C., Black Repertory Company and as a consultant in black music to the Smithsonian Institution.

My Thoughts in Writing

1. Trace the changes in Reagon's view of black music as her essay progresses. How does each change relate to her initial view of this traditional African-American form of expression? How does she finally come to define it?

2. Where does Reagon first mention making her own changes to traditional music? What was the effect of this experience? What did she learn as a result of this experience about the purpose of the tradition and the role of change in maintaining the tradition?

3. What types of black music does Reagon mention in the essay? Why is it important that she mentions more than one type? What function does black music serve in the community? Although Reagon does not list them outright, what suggestions does she give for keeping the tradition alive?

————————— ✦ —————————

In the early 1960s, I was in college at Albany State. My major interests were music and biology. In music I was a contralto soloist with the choir, studying Italian arias and German lieder. The Black music I sang was of three types:

(1) Spirituals sung by the college choir. These were arranged by such people as Nathaniel Dett and William Dawson and had major injections of European musical harmony and composition. (2) Rhythm 'n' Blues, music done by and for Blacks in social settings. This included the music of bands at proms, juke boxes, and football game songs. (3) Church music; gospel was a major part of Black church music by the time I was in college. I was a soloist with the gospel choir.

Prior to the gospel choir, introduced in my church when I was twelve, was many years' experience with unaccompanied music—Black choral singing, hymns, lined out by strong song leaders with full, powerful, richly ornate congregational responses. These hymns were offset by upbeat, clapping call-and-response songs.

I saw people in church sing and pray until they shouted. I knew *that* music as a part of a cultural expression that was powerful enough to take people from their conscious selves to a place where the physical and intellectual being worked in harmony with the spirit. I enjoyed and needed that experience. The music of the church was an integral part of the cultural world into which I was born.

5   Outside of church, I saw music as good, powerful sounds you made or listened to. Rhythm and blues—you danced to; music of the college choir—you clapped after the number was finished.

The Civil Rights Movement changed my view of music. It was after my first march. I began to sing a song and in the course of singing changed the song so that it made sense for that particular moment. Although I was not consciously aware of it, this was one of my earliest experiences with how my music was supposed to *function*. This music was to be integrative of and consistent with everything I was doing at that time; it was to be tied to activities that went beyond artistic affairs such as concerts, dances, and church meetings.

The next level of awareness came while in jail. I had grown up in a rural area outside the city limits, riding a bus to public school or driving to college. My life had been a pretty consistent, balanced blend of church, school, and proper upbringing. I was aware of a Black educated class that taught me in high school and college, of taxi cabs I never rode in, and of people who used buses I never boarded. I went to school with their children.

In jail with me were all these people. All ages. In my section were women from about thirteen to eighty years old. Ministers' wives and teachers and teachers' wives who had only nodded at me or clapped at a concert or spoken to my mother. A few people from my classes. A large number of people who rode segregated city buses. One or two women who had been drinking along the two-block stretch of Little Harlem as the march went by. Very quickly, clashes arose: around age, who would have authority, what was proper behavior?

The Albany Movement was already a singing movement, and we took the songs to jail. There the songs I had sung because they made me feel good or because they said what I thought about a specific issue did something. I would start a song and everybody would join in. After the song, the differences among us would not be as great. Somehow, making a song required an expression of that which was common to us all. The songs did not feel like the same songs I had sung in college. This music was like an instrument, like holding a tool in your hand.

I found that although I was younger than many of the women in my section of the jail, I was asked to take on leadership roles. First as a song leader and then in most other matters concerning the group, especially in discussions, or when speaking with prison officials. 10

I fell in love with that kind of music. I saw that to define music as something you listen to, something that pleases you, is very different from defining it as an instrument with which you can drive a point. In both instances, you can have the same song. But using it as an instrument makes it a different kind of music.

The next level of awareness occurred during the first mass meeting after my release from jail. I was asked to lead the song that I had changed after the first march. When I opened my mouth and began to sing, there was a force and power within myself I had never heard before. Somehow this music—music I could use as an instrument to do things with, music that was mine to shape and change so that it made the statement I needed to make—released a kind of power and required a level of concentrated energy I did not know I had. I liked the feeling.

For several years, I worked with the Movement eventually doing Civil Rights songs with the Freedom Singers. The Freedom Singers used the songs, interspersed with narrative, to convey the story of the Civil Rights Movement's struggles. The songs were more powerful than spoken conversation. They became a major way of making people who were not on the scene feel the intensity of what was happening in the south. Hopefully, they would move the people to take a stand, to organize support groups or participate in various projects.

The Georgia Sea Island Singers, whom I first heard at the Newport Festival, were a major link. Bessie Jones, coming from within twenty miles of Albany, Georgia, had a repertoire

and song-leading style I recognized from the churches I had
grown up in. She, along with John Davis, would talk about
songs that Black people had sung as slaves and what those
songs meant in terms of their struggle to be free. The songs
did not sound like the spirituals I had sung in college choirs;
they sounded like the songs I had grown up with in church.
There I had been fold the songs had to do with worship of Jesus Christ.

15   The next few years I spent focusing on three compo-
nents: (1) The music I had found in the Civil Rights Movement. (2) Songs of the Georgia Sea Island Singers and other
traditional groups, and the ways in which those songs were
linked to the struggles of Black peoples at earlier times. (3)
Songs of the church that now sounded like those traditional
songs and came close to having, for many people, the same
kind of freeing power.

There was another experience that helped to shape my
present-day use of music. After getting out of jail, the mother
of the church my father pastored was at the mass meeting.
She prayed, a prayer I had heard hundreds of times. I had focused on its sound, tune, rhythm, chant, whether the moans
came at the proper pace and intensity. That morning I heard
every word that she said. She did not have to change one word
of prayer she had been praying for much of her Christian life
for me to know she was addressing the issues we were facing
at that moment. More than her personal prayer, it felt like an
analysis of the Albany, Georgia, Black community.

My collection, study, and creation of Black music has
been, to a large extent, about freeing the sounds and the words
and the messages from casings in which they have been put,
about hearing clearly what the music has to say about Black
people and their struggle.

When I first began to search, I looked for what was then being called folk music, rather than for other Black forms, such as
jazz, rhythm and blues, or gospel. It slowly dawned on me that
during the Movement we had used all those forms. When we
were relaxing in the office, we made up songs using popular
rhythm and blues tunes; songs based in rhythm and blues also
came out of jails, especially from the sit-in movement and the

march to Selma, Alabama. "Oh Wallace, You Never Can Jail Us All" is an example from Selma. "You Better Leave Segregation Alone" came out of the Nashville Freedom Rides and was based on a bit by Little Willie John, "You Better Leave My Kitten Alone." Gospel choirs became the major musical vehicle in the urban center of Birmingham, with the choir led by Carlton Reese. There was also a gospel choir in the Chicago work, as well as an instrumental ensemble led by Ben Branch. Jazz had not been a strong part of my musical life. I began to hear it as I traveled north. Thelonious Monk and Charlie Mingus played on the first SNCC benefit at Carnegie Hall. I heard of and then heard Coltrane. Then I began to pick up the pieces that had been laid by Charlie Parker and Coleman Hawkins and whole lifetimes of music. This music had no words. But, it had power, intensity, and movement under various degrees of pressure; it had vocal texture and color. I could feel that the music knew how it felt to be Black and Angry, Black and Down, Black and Loved, Black and Fighting.

I now believe that Black music exists in every place where Black people run, every corner where they live, every level on which they struggle. We have been here a long while, in many situations. It takes all that we have created to sing our song. I believe that Black musicians/artists have a responsibility to be conscious of their world and to let their consciousness be heard in their songs. 20

And we need it all—blues, gospel, ballads, children's games, dance, rhythms, jazz, lovesongs, topical songs—doing what it has always done. We need Black music that functions in relation to the people and community who provide the nurturing compost that makes its creation and continuation possible.

from *Growing Up in Cairo*
JEHAN SADAT

Born in 1934 in Cairo, Jehan Sadat was the daughter of an Egyptian civil servant and an English mother. She is the widow of Egyptian president Anwar al-Sadat, who was assassinatied in 1981. Her writings often reflect both the struggle between culture and personal identity and the value of cultural traditions in the life of family and community.

My Thoughts in Writing

1. Although Sadat's parents were of different religions, this was not the reason her grandparents disapproved of her parents' marriage. Why did they disapprove of the union? What moves them to eventually accept it?
2. What does the change in this family's tradition do to the family as a whole? Who is affected the most? How does this changing tradition reflect life in Cairo at that time? Use the text to illustrate your point.
3. As one tradition changes, how are others affected? Make a list of the traditions Sadat mentions in the essay. Then, discuss how each tradition was affected by her parents' marriage. Explain whether the effects were positive or negative.

———————— ✦ ————————

I did not know until I was eleven that my name was Jehan, a Persian name picked out by my father which means "the world." My mother, who was English, had nicknamed me Jean, and that was what I was called by my father, an employee at the Ministry of Health, by my teachers at the Christian missionary school I attended, and by my friends. It was not at all strange for me or my classmates to have European names. I had friends named Mimi and Fifi, Helen and Betty. Egyptians had greatly admired European ways since our leader Muhammad Ali had opened Egypt to foreign influence one hundred years before, believing the Europeans to be much more advanced. But it was strange that I did not even know my proper name until I received my primary-school certificate before moving on to secondary school.

"Who is Jehan?" I asked the teacher, seeing it written on my certificate over my address.

"You," she told me.

I ran home to my mother. "What is my name?" I asked her.

"In school now you are Jehan," she told me. "In our family   5
you are Jean." And to this day that is what my sister and
brothers call me. I was born on Roda Island, one of two islands in the Nile
linked by bridges to Cairo in the east and Giza to the west. My
island of Roda was a lovely area of gardens and gracious
peach limestone villas populated by middle-class Egyptian
families. The neighboring island of Zamalek was fancier,
home to many British families and those of the Egyptian upper class. The Gezira Sporting Club on Zamalek, to which my
family did not belong, boasted cricket pitches and polo fields,
tennis courts and swimming pools and a bar at which liquor
was served. The Gezira Club was in another world to me as a
child, and to many other Egyptians as well. King Farouk was a
member there, as were many of the foreign families, but there
was a membership quota for Egyptians.

I was the third of four children in my family, and the first
girl. A great space of age spread between my brothers and me.
Magdi was ten years older, Ali seven. My mother, I was told,
had yearned to have a girl, to comb a daughter's hair and em-
broider her dresses. The day of my birth was a cause of great
celebration in our house, compounded by an *'allawa*, a raise in
pay my father took that very same day from his government
job. From the beginning, I was considered by my parents to be
a good omen. Twenty-one months later, my sister Dalia was
born and our family was complete.

We were all very light-skinned, a legacy not only from my
English mother but on my father's side as well. My father's father was a Sa'idi, an Upper Egyptian from the tall, usually
dark-skinned tribe descended from pure Pharaonic stock. Yet
my grandfather too had been fair with blue eyes. His children—my father, my uncle and my two Egyptian aunts—were
also fair, and, like all Egyptian families, we were all very close.

When I was a baby we lived with our relatives in one house,
splitting up when I was five years old. But no one moved very
far away. My bachelor Uncle Mustafa lived just one house away
with his divorced sister, 'Aziza, it being his responsibility as a
brother to look after her and her young daughter, 'Aida. I visited my Auntie 'Aziza, or Auntie Zouzou as she was nicknamed,

every afternoon, and often she came to our home in the evenings. She was my favorite aunt and my Egyptian mother, showering me with affection and spoiling me.

10   After my Uncle Mustafa finally married at thirty-eight, Aunt Zouzou continued to live with him and his new wife, for it was improper then for a woman to live alone. I'm sure she was very lonely, but she continued to refuse many offers of marriage, fearing that her daughter might be mistreated by a stepfather.

My other aunt, Fatima, whom we fondly called Auntie Batta—Auntie "Duck"—lived just outside Cairo on the Pyramids Road. She was not as affectionate as Auntie Zouzou, but she was a very strong woman. After my grandmother died, Auntie Batta effectively took her place. It was to Auntie Batta's house that the whole family went to break the fast on the first day of Ramadan, and to her that they went to seek advice. Auntie Batta was married to Husni Abu Zaid, an official in the Wafd nationalist party who had served as governor of both Munufiyya province and Minia province. Uncle Husni had a government car, quite a symbol of prosperity at the time, and I loved to drive with him around Cairo. With its official license plate and the flag of Munufiyya fluttering on the fender, the car prompted all the soldiers who saw it to salute. As a little girl, I liked to imagine they were saluting me.

"The mother of the world," the historian Ibn el-Khaldun had called Cairo in the fourteenth century. As a child growing up in Roda, it was easy to see why. Everywhere were the signs of Cairo's rich past. Directly across the Nile to the east was Coptic Cairo, which for more than fifteen hundred years had been the center of Egyptian Christian art and religion. On my way to school I could see the spires of the fourth-century Abu Serga Church, built on the spot where it is believed the family of Jesus stayed during their flight into Egypt. Beyond Abu Serga, I could sometimes make out the thin Ottoman minarets of the Alabaster Mosque, built by Muhammad 'Ali in the nineteenth century. Still farther along was the Old City founded by the Fatimids in 973, and el-Azhar Mosque and University. El-Azhar is the oldest university in the world, and attracts more than 100,000 students from countries as far away as Mauritania and Indonesia. All who come are students of Islam, for though el-Azhar is old, our religion is still young and growing. From the other side of Roda, I could look across the Nile to the west and see the river gardens of the rich merchants who lived in Giza, beyond to the campus of Cairo University, and to the Pyramids Road, which, if followed to the end, terminated at the Farafra Oasis in the Libyan Desert. On a clear day when no dust or sand blew, I could make out the tips of the Great Pyramids themselves. And always in the air, five times a day, I could hear the beautiful voices of the muezzins high up in the minarets of Cairo's thousands of mosques, calling the believers in Islam to prayer.

How lovely and quiet Roda Island was during my childhood. Everyone had green gardens, and between the villas on both sides of the island you could always see the Nile passing. In 1933, the population of Egypt was around 15 million, and the population of Cairo less than one million.

My mother must have been very brave to leave her native land of England to come live in Egypt. My father must have been brave also to have married a foreigner. Such a marriage was not against our religion of Islam, for the children of a Muslim man will always themselves be Muslim. It was forbidden only for a Muslim woman to marry into another religion, for her children would have to bear the religion of their father. No. My grandparents' objection to their marriage was not religious, but one of family tradition.

My father, Safwat Raouf, had met my mother, Gladys Charles Cotrell, in 1923 in Sheffield, England, where he was studying medicine at the University of Sheffield and she was a music teacher. Their love was very strong from the beginning. It had to be, for a marriage had already been arranged in Cairo between my father and his cousin. "No one in our family has ever married a foreigner," my grandfather wrote to my father in England. "I will not give you permission to marry this Englishwoman."

My grandparents were well used to the British, of course, for there were many, many British in Egypt at that time. Since the 1800s more than ten thousand British troops had been stationed in Egypt to "protect" our government. The British High

Commissioner, Lord Cromer, was effectively ruling the country. Britain and France controlled Egypt's finances. Even Egypt's shares in the Suez Canal, completed in 1869, had had to be sold to the British by our then debt-ridden Khedive Isma'il. It was certainly not uncommon to see the British and many other foreigners in Cairo. But it was difficult for my conservative grandparents to adjust to new ways.

"If you do not allow this marriage, I will not eat until I am dead," my father wrote back to my grandfather. My grandfather was just as stubborn. "I will not give my permission," he replied. And back and forth the letters went until my grandmother grew worried that my father really might harm himself or, just as bad, not come back to Egypt at all. "You must give your permission," she told my grandfather. "Is it not better to welcome our son and his wife home to Egypt than to force him to live in a country foreign to our ways?"

Reluctantly my grandfather had agreed, and my grandmother had sent my mother the traditional Egyptian engagement present of jewelry, in this case a diamond ring and a diamond-and-sapphire necklace she had inherited from her grandfather, along with money for a honeymoon. My mother and father were married in a civil ceremony in England, and when my father returned home with my mother three years later it was with my brother, who had been born in Liverpool. As was the custom then, my parents moved into my grandparents' house on Roda Island. Quickly, my grandparents grew to love my mother, though it must not have been easy for any of them. Our society was more conservative then. And my mother's ways, indeed, were strange.

20   She never ate Egyptian food, but insisted on the Sudanese cook making a separate meal for her of boiled meat, boiled vegetables, boiled everything. The rest of the family ate the usual Egyptian fare: grilled pigeon; grilled fish; lamb kebab and *kufta*, spiced patties of minced lamb; *wara einab*, grape leaves stuffed with rice and minced meat; *molokhia*, a thick soup made of a minced green leaf and chicken stock; *bamia*, okra sautéed with butter, onion, garlic and tomato paste in broth, served almost always with rice, and different kinds of beans and salads. But my mother would eat boiled mutton and potatoes with mint sauce.

Breakfast was different for us also. In the morning, and indeed for all meals, Egyptians traditionally eat *ful medammes*—fava beans boiled into a thick paste with spices and topped with a fried egg. At our house we had cornflakes, boiled eggs, and thinly sliced toast instead of *'aish*, our flat, unleavened bread, along with jam my mother had made. Tea every afternoon at four was sacred, and she would serve us English tea instead of the sweet mint tea Egyptians drink, and wonderful British cakes, biscuits and sweets she'd made for us to eat. They were delicious, really, especially the lemon curd preserve which we didn't have in Egypt at all.

We shared our house with another family who lived in an apartment upstairs, and, to their wonder and the wonder of our other neighbors, my mother would bring a lovely pine tree into the house at Christmas and decorate it with shiny stars and balls, topping it off with a figure of Father Christmas. Nadia and Tahani, the children who lived upstairs, as well as other children in the neighborhood would rush to see our tree, because very few Egyptian families celebrated Christmas and none had ever seen a Christmas tree. Our friends envied us not only because of our tree and the delicious Christmas pudding my mother made, but because we received gifts as well.

It was difficult for my mother to live so far away from her country. During World War II all communication was cut off between England and Egypt. She heard no news from her family at all and was very worried. One day I found her crying in her room when I returned from school.

"What is wrong with Mummy?" I asked Betty, a friend of my mother's who had been visiting.

"She has just learned that her father passed away," Betty   25
told me. "Her family has sent her some money and his watch." A few months later she lost her mother as well.

I felt so sorry for her. I would never have wanted to be away so long from my family. But she did not want to leave her children or her husband to go for a visit. For thirty years she did not return to England, and when she did she could not recognize the streets or even find her family house in Sheffield. To locate her family, my mother put a notice in the local newspaper, saying what hotel she was staying in. That afternoon her only living sister and other relatives rushed to see her. It was a very moving meeting after such a long separation, and the newspaper in Sheffield published a story about it.

My mother did not raise us to be British. Not at all. At home we all spoke Arabic, which she had learned to speak as well. She was not a proselytizer, so she did not influence us in any way from our Muslim traditions. But still it was a little bit confusing to me as a small child. My mother kept a crucifix of the prophet Jesus over her bed, and sometimes I would see her kneeling before it in prayer, her hands clasped together in the Christian manner though as small children we did not yet pray, I knew that the Muslims prayed differently, standing with the arms outstretched and prostrating themselves on the ground. I was confused by this difference between my mother and the rest of the family.

"Why are you Christian while we are all Muslim?" I asked her one afternoon after a classmate questioned me about it.

"Nobody chooses their religion," she explained to me in a very sweet way. "We are all what we are born to be. The important thing to remember is that all religions have just one God. It does not matter how we worship Him so long as we have faith."

30   But still it bothered me. My mother's Christian ways made me think more deeply about our Muslim traditions which others just took for granted. At the Coptic missionary school that all the children attended, the only primary school on Roda, the Christian teacher read stories to us several times a week from the Bible, stories about all the prophets and about Jesus Christ. Every morning before classes began there was a Christian prayer service, which the teacher had told us we did not have to attend if we did not want to. So I didn't, staying at my desk in the classroom while all the other students went to the service, including my sister, who was too young to understand.

"Why don't you come with me?" my sister said.

"It is for the Christians and we are Muslim," I told her.

"But you will make the teacher angry," she said.

I didn't care. "I am not going to go listen to a priest just to please the teacher," I insisted.

But my sister was right. The teacher became cruel toward   35
me, making me stand in the corner with my face to the wall
every day during our recreational period.

"Your sister comes to prayers. So do the other students,
both of whose parents are Muslim," the teacher said to me.
"Why must you be different?"

"I am not a Christian," I would reply. And back I would go
into the corner.

I was only eight at the time, and after three weeks of this I
told my father how cruelly I felt the teacher was treating me.
The next morning he came to see the British headmistress.

"I do not want either of my daughters to attend the Christian prayer service," he told her. "That is not their religion and
the teacher is pressuring them."

The headmistress was evidently shocked when my father   40
told her how severely I was being treated. She must have spoken to my teacher, because after my father's visit she treated
me very kindly. From then on both Dalia and I stayed at our
desks while the others went to chapel.

My mother never converted to Islam, though many of her
British friends who were married to Egyptians did. Conver-
sion was very simple, requiring registration as a Muslim at el-
Azhar Mosque with two people as witnesses, and the recita-
tion five times of the profession of faith: "I testify that there is
no god but God, and Muhammad is His messenger." Her
reluctance to convert perplexed my aunts and uncle. "Why
doesn't Gladys change her religion?" my father's family and
friends used to ask. But my father loved my mother very much
and never wanted to pressure her. Instead, we would follow
our tradition and holidays with my father's family. And my
mother would share somewhat, even fasting a few days during
Ramadan to encourage us. We were a Muslim family with a
Christian mother.

She was not a typical Egyptian mother, protectively hovering over her children. Not at all. When we fell playing games
in the garden, our aunts would always rush to pick us up. "Let
them get up by themselves," my mother would say. Unlike
many Egyptian mothers, who, after washing their children's
hair, for example, made their children stay inside until their

hair was dry, my mother would say, "Nonsense. Go outside and let the wind and sun dry it."

Many Egyptian mothers sat at night with their children until they fell asleep, then left a light burning for them so that they would not be frightened if they awoke. My mother disapproved of that, thinking it made the children dependent and soft. Instead she went in quite the other direction. Every night before we went to bed she made us go out into the black, black garden alone and find our way around it three times in the dark. That way, she said, we would learn not to be afraid of being alone and not be afraid of the dark. And she was right.

Our home had a very warm, loving atmosphere. Every day my father returned from his office at two, the time all government offices closed for the day, with packets of chocolates, a new French cheese or a present of smoked tongue for us. Our main meal was at midday, after which all Cairenes including us, took naps until four or five. After his nap, my father never went out again the way many other Egyptian men did—going to the cafés to drink coffee, play backgammon or smoke the nargilehs or water pipes. Either we all went out together or he stayed home.

45   Sometimes on Friday, our Sabbath day, my father would take us to the Old City, marked by the Bab el-Metwalli, or Gate of the Holy Man, named after the Sufi sheikh who reportedly sat there centuries before, performing miracles for passersby. For all that Cairo was my hometown, I never ceased to marvel at the sights and the exotic history that made up my city. The streets of the Old City, far too narrow for automobiles, were choked instead with the traffic of horses, donkeys and even people laden down with loads of fresh vegetables, firesticks, vases of copper and brass to be sold in the bustling Khan el-Khalili bazaar. Cairo had been the greatest trading center in the world for centuries, and it was here in the caravanserai of the Khan el-Khalili that medieval traders from all over the Arab world had unloaded their camel trains. It was near here also that the Fatimid sultans had kept a zoo for the giraffes, ostriches and elephants sent to them as tribute from kingdoms in Africa.

The twelve thousand shops of the Khan el-Khalili were filled with remnants of the past being used in the present. My parents often took us through the dark, winding streets to the silver and gold market, located in the very heart of the bazaar so as to protect it from invaders. There my sister and I could buy silver bracelets for ten cents. While my mother stopped by the spice market to buy mint, thyme and sage for her British sauces, we children would strain to hear the clanking finger cymbals of the roving juice seller as children had for centuries, then pester our father to buy us glasses of the cold black syrupy sweet juice of the *tamarbindy*.

Sample Student Essay

The Essence of Traditions

ANGELIQUE WURPEL

My family has always been close-knit, and this shows when we gather for holidays. We celebrate the holidays to be sure, but what we are truly celebrating is the fact that we are a family. Our holiday get-togethers are usually very happy occasions, with children running and playing and the adults talking and joking around together. This past year has been different, because my Uncle Sam and my Grandfather John have both passed away. Now everyone seems to be looking at the places where they used to sit instead of watching the kids at play. Everyone misses my uncle and my grandfather, and although I know things can never be the same, we must once again make our holidays the celebrations of family they once were.

To much of the family, Sam and John were the focal points. John and his wife, Sara, had six children, two of whom were Sam and my mother, Lisa. He lived through World War II and D day. He had many stories to tell, and he often shared them with us on holidays. After the war, he became an integral part of his community. He founded the Little Devils (a bugle and drum corps), a color guard, and a drill team.

Sam, my mother's brother, had two children, Rebecca and Nathan. They are both in their twenties now. He was an electrician by trade, but he did a little bit of everything. He was a great cook, and he often contributed a dish or two to Thanksgiving and Easter dinners. Everyone misses his cooking. He always had a video camera with him, and when I was little, I can remember him taping me and the rest of the hoard of grandchildren as we played together during our family holiday gatherings. Sam had an air of confidence about him and he was known for his sharp wit.

For Thanksgiving dinner, Sam usually brought the turkey. He would prepare it at his home, and then bring it to cook at my aunt's house. It was but one contribution, but it sure helped. Now my aunt has to cook everything herself. This past Thanksgiving almost didn't happen because it occurred less than three weeks after Sam had passed away. No one was quite ready to celebrate in the middle of all that sadness. Nevertheless, we still had dinner—even though the turkey tasted like ashes instead of the culinary masterpiece it usually was. After dinner, Sam was almost always found sleeping on one of the couches somewhere in the house. But this past year, I was the one happily dozing off, and everyone joked that I had taken Sam's place. I don't know if this is a good thing or a bad thing. But if there has to be change—and there does now—I like to think of this one as good because filling my uncle's shoes (or couch) is a pleasure to me.

The February following my uncle's death, my grandfather John passed away, and everyone was upset all over again. His family is much more extensive, with relatives living all the way up in northeastern Pennsylvania. At the holidays, he was missed just as much as Sam, if not more. Easter had such a sad feel to it because not one, but two favored men were missing from the family holiday table. I got the feeling that no one wanted to see anyone else when very few people came to Easter dinner that day.

The children's egg hunt was just as it had always been, the small kids not really knowing the losses of the past seven months. The bigger kids raced around as usual, while the smaller ones were being led around by their older siblings or parents. This was the only part of the day that remained untouched by the grief of the past year. The saddest realization of the day came when Sara, who used to use John's failing health as an excuse to leave, just waited until the splendid dinner was over to say that she was tired and to take her leave amid sympathetic and parting words.

These days everyone is still getting over the loss of John and his son Sam. These wounds will eventually heal, but it is going to take some time, and not all of us will heal at the same pace. Nevertheless, we'll wait for the sad ones to remember the good times we've had in the past and to think of the good times we can have together in the future. We'll wait for them to remember that they still have the rest of the family here for them. Family is the essence of traditions, and I hope we can all remember that when the holidays come around again this year.

My Thoughts in Writing

1. Early in her introduction, Wurpel redefines her family's holiday celebrations. How does she view them? What proof does she give of her way of seeing her family's celebrations?
2. What has happened to change the Wurpel family traditions? What types of changes have taken place? How does Wurpel feel about these changes?
3. In the end, Wurpel seems to be trying to call her relatives back to their traditions. How does she do this? What does she emphasize?

The Readings Come Together

1. Compare Glaser's and Tapahonso's poems. How are both poems tributes to traditions? What is being said about the way things were done in the past and how traditions change over time? Do the poems contain the same message about changing traditions? Use the poems to explain your answer.
2. Wurpel tells us that her family celebrated holidays together at home and that in a way they were more a celebration of family than holiday celebrations. Based on what Giovanni says in her essay, do you think Giovanni would accept or reject the way the Wurpels celebrated their holidays? Explain your answer using both essays to illustrate your point.
3. In what way are the essays by Sadat, Reagon, and Rohter similar? What do you learn from them about the role of tradition in the lives of individuals and communities?
4. There is a sense of nostalgia in both Wurpel's essay and Tapahonso's poem. How do both pieces convey a longing for the past? Does one convey acceptance of the present more so than the other does? If so, which one and how? If not, illustrate your point by addressing specific areas of each work.
5. In Sadat's essay, she details how a change to one tradition has a kind of trickle-down effect. How is this similar to what happens to Wurpel's family following the deaths of two important family members and the Carnival in Rio when commercialism is introduced?

There's Something More out There

Part I

At-Home Activity

Prelude Prewriting. Refer to your list (prepared in the previous chapter) of traditional gatherings engaged in by your family or community. Choose two or three and through interviews with family or community members determine which traditions have changed over time. Try to determine how they have changed and why. Record the information you gather in your journal.

Part II

Classroom Storytelling Session

A Room full of tradition: Discovering the past in today. Looking for Likeness, Sharing Difference. Together with your classmates, create a list of those traditional gatherings that have changed somewhat over time. Discuss the effects of these changes to tradition. Compare and contrast how your traditions have changed and how they have stayed the same.

Part III

Journal Entry

Option 1. Choose one tradition from Part I to focus on. Then, write a complete journal entry about that tradition. If the tradition has changed, explain how and why. In addition, try to determine how the changes have affected your family and the role of the tradition itself. If you would rather write about a tradition that remains the same each and every year, then you must explain the reason(s) for its constancy. How does your family or community maintain the tradition in the same way year after year? Why do you think this occurs? How does it affect the tradition itself?

Option 2. Choose a classmate whose family or community engages in a tradition similar to, but also different from, one that your family or community engages in. How are the traditions alike? How are they different? What do the similarities and differences reveal about your different groups? Do you share the same values and assumptions? Do you use the traditions for the same purpose? What is that purpose? If not, how do your purposes differ? What explanations can you give for the similarities and difference(s)?

Part IV

Writing Assignment

Using a study of one or more of the reading selections provided in this chapter, create an essay based on your journal assignment. In your introduction, you should make clear whether you are studying similarities, differences, or both similarities and differences. In addition, your thesis should indicate the purpose of your comparison-contrast: do you want to make the unfamiliar familiar, show what is fresh and new about the familiar, persuade readers that the new way of tradition in your family or community is better than the old or vice versa, or to make the reader better understand the nature of the traditions under study in your essay?

Millennium Folklore

THE FOLKLORE FOCUS

Folklore in the New Century

Each year, at the close of summer, the Philadelphia Folk Festival takes place. People come from across the country to be a part of this fun-filled family and friends event. Many participants camp out on the festival grounds, equipped with enough provisions to last the duration of the festival. They return year after year, clearing their schedules to make room for this celebration of, this emersion in, folklore. There are quilters, woodworkers, crafters, and cooks at work from dawn until dusk, exhibiting their talents and sharing their knowledge with the audience. Skillful storytellers are in abundance, entertaining crowds of all ages and setting an example for the next generation. Traditional and contemporary folk music can be heard virtually wherever you are on the festival grounds, and it's hard to resist joining in when it comes to the folk and square dancing. Such tributes to folklore's longevity are not rare, and the enthusiasm exhibited for these occasions attests to the rich taste of our traditions. Folk festivals, conferences, gatherings, and exhibits are testaments to the value of folklore. When coupled with the abundant folklore revealed and demonstrated during the numerous specific cultural celebrations that occur annually (like the Native American, African American, and Hispanic American festivals held throughout this country each year), there seems to be ample evidence that folklore is alive and well even today.

However, there are those who would disagree with such a thought. They would profess that folklore is a dying thing and those who engage in it, a vanishing breed. Since folklore exists only by word of mouth or customary example, a folklore naysayer might argue that folklore quickly will be made ineffectual, given all technology allows us to do without effort, without talking, without seeing each other; that our desire for all that is speedy and technological will soon overshadow our love of and patience for grandma's recipes or our neighbor's workshop creations. What do you think? Will the heritage and self-knowledge contained in our folk traditions take a back seat to the ease and comfort technology offers? Those of us who study folklore and live by it are curious to know: what will be the fate of folklore in the new century?

Your own folklore work should have shown you much about folklore's role in your own life and perhaps its value to this multicultural world in which we live. How do you think it stands up against today's way of life? What role, if any, will folklore play in the coming decades? How would you define the relationship between our traditional means of expression and ways of knowing and more contemporary methods of communication and knowledge attainment? As you review the work you have done in the previous chapters, as you compare what you once knew of folklore with what you now know, think about what folklore means to you and what you have learned it means to others. Study what this chapter's writers have to say about our multicultural, multitraditional world, about folklore's role in the past and the present, about folklore's influence on individuals and community members. And, finally, from the information you gather, try clearly to define your position on the state of folklore in the world today. Which side—"alive and well" or "taking its last breath"— will you take in the great debate over folklore's fate?

This chapter encourages you carefully to consider the future of folklore. The readings selected for this chapter and the questions that follow them will help you do this. Each selection centers on the possibility of tradition and traditional values in an ever-changing technological world. Together, they illustrate a variety of opinions on the matter and work to

show the seriousness of the subject. The questions that precede each selection require you to think deeply about what individual writers have to say about the role tradition will play
in the years to come—especially where their particular communities or a world community is concerned. Once more, pay
attention to the devices writers use to make their selections
come to life. How is sensory detail used to the selection's advantage? How does the writer's tone reflect the overall meaning the selection conveys? What other narrative techniques
does the writer employ to make his or her point clear? Your
careful analysis of these selections and the varying viewpoints
they present will help you come to your own conclusions
about the state of family and community folklore and will
prepare you for writing about your own feelings regarding
the future of folk traditions.

The Blues Is Dying in the Place It Was Born

RICK BRAGG

Born and raised in Alabama, Rick Bragg is a Pulitzer
Prize–winning national correspondent for the *New York Times*
and author of the best-selling book *All Over but the Shoutin'*.
In addition to his more than fifty writing awards, Bragg is a
two-time winner of the American Society of Newspaper Edi-
tors Distinguished Writing Award.

My Thoughts in Writing

1. According to the author and the people he interviewed,
   what is "the blues"? Develop a definition based on the
   "blues" descriptions provided in the essay.
2. Where does such music still get played? Why is this kind
   of airtime not enough to keep the blues tradition alive and
   well? What else is needed?

3. What evidence does the author provide that the "blues is fading from the very place it was born"? What happens when traditions, like the blues, die out?

4. Does Bragg suggest or imply a method that might work to maintain this tradition and others like it?

———————————— ✦ ————————————

The blues is, when polio freezes your fingers and shrivels your legs, you play a baby-blue Epiphone guitar on your lap in a wheelchair, chording the strings with a butter knife. CeDell Davis, crippled by that disease when he was 10, almost 63 years ago, lives inside the blues.

The blues is, when you find the fine, big woman of your dreams, she dies in your arms of a heart attack just before dawn. James (T-Model) Ford, who swears he would have married her, is wed to the blues.

The blues is, when the searing light from your welder's torch slowly, gradually burns much of the sight from your eyes, you sit on your porch in the cool damp of the afternoon and sing to the rhythms in your own mind, then go into town for a bottle of Wild Irish Rose. Paul Jones, who knows the narrow roads in Belzoni so well he does not need to see that much to drive, has surrendered to the blues.

"I believe in God, but the Devil, he's got power, too," said Mr. Jones, who, with Mr. Davis, Mr. Ford and a scattering of others, is among the last of the Delta bluesmen who still live in the cradle of the blues. "Most of what you sing about is suffering."

5   Musicians who were not born here, who have not had their spirits or their bodies broken, who have never looked at these endless cotton fields and hated them, can never truly play the blues, said Mr. Ford, who now lives in Greenville, Miss., and Mr. Davis, who lives across the Mississippi River in Pine Bluff, Ark. Outsiders might play a tune from the Delta, Mr. Jones said, but there is no feeling in it.

"It's just," he said, "something you hear."

But here in the Delta, where most of the legendary juke joints have slowly shut their doors and most of the bluesmen have died off or moved away, the blues is fading from the very place it was born, say the people who play it and others who live here.

They know their music survives, in the music collections of yuppies, in college seminars on folk culture, in festivals and franchised venues like the House of Blues, B. B. King's clubs and others in the United States, Asia and Europe.

But there is little live music left, the bluesmen say, at the source. They play at festivals and the few weekend clubs that have endured, but even on the jukeboxes in the surviving bars and fish houses there is little Delta country blues. Hip-hop thuds from cars. Gospel, country and soul music, sister to the blues, dominate the radio.

"I made $2,000 in one night in Japan," Mr. Jones said, but   10
here he may make $300, if the phone rings at all. Like Mr. Davis and Mr. Ford, he has been recorded by a label in Water Valley, Miss., called Fat Possum Records, which also aids the men in booking shows here and around the world. No one is getting rich, but, Mr. Jones wonders, if he had not been picked up by that small label, would he have slowly disappeared too?

Matthew Johnson, who was one of the founders of Fat Possum 10 years ago, said he never wanted to be a folklorist; he "just wanted to make records that rock." CeDell Davis says crack cocaine and the culture it bred turned the already tough juke joints into slaughterhouses over the last 15 years, driving people away and all but silencing the small live shows that are now mostly folklore.

But the people of the Delta will come back to the blues, he said.

"The blues is about peoples, and as long as there's peoples, there will be blues," Mr. Davis said. "The blues tells a story. Hip-hop don't tell no story. It don't tell no story about women, men, trains, buses, cars, birds, alleys, stores."

"THE BLUES IS ABOUT THINGS"

When you sing the blues, here in one of the poorest, most unchanging corners of the country, you hand everybody who listens a piece of your pain, fear and hopelessness, until there is such a tiny piece left, you can live with it. Sometimes, as Mr.

Jones showed when he sang on a side porch one afternoon, it sounds a lot like church.

> Take away my sins and give me grace
> Take away my sins and give me grace
> Oh angels, Oh my Lord
> Wish I was in heaven sittin' down.

15   It is the very authenticity of the blues that endangers it. Mae Smith grew up in Lula, Mississippi, where a man named Frank Frost pushed a broom at her school. Later, she found his name in a history of the blues.

"I thought he was the town drunk," said Ms. Smith, who helps run the Delta Blues Museum in Clarksdale, Mississippi, and holds the title of interpretation specialist. Many blues players live hard and die in obscurity, and a piece of Delta history vanishes.

The Delta, like the blues, belongs to black people, the people here say, though many do not own enough of it to root a vine. It was their sweat that cleared its vast forests and transformed a 19th-century jungle into the richest farmland on earth.

It lies in the deltas of the Mississippi and Yazoo rivers, an indistinct triangle of vast fields, islands of trees and small towns extending south from Memphis for about 200 miles, covering an area about 70 miles wide on both sides of the Mississippi.

No other place, bluesmen say, could have nurtured the blues. What other place saw such toil, such pain?

20   What other place could produce a man like T-Model Ford, whose ankles are scarred from two years on a Tennessee chain gang, who walks with a cane because a jack slipped and a truck crushed one leg, who sings about pistol fights, abandonment, murder and adultery, and smiles and smiles?

BACK-DOOR MAN

In Greenville, in a small house behind the funeral home, the amplifier crackles like lightning in a box as he plugs in the guitar he calls Gold Nanny, sister to Black Nanny.

> I should have left you, baby
> Gone on back to Mexico

> I kept messin' with you, baby
> Now you got me on the killin' floor.

Some days, a bus full of Japanese tourists will roll up. They take his picture, as they would photograph any other endangered species.

He did not sell his soul, as legend says Robert Johnson did, to master the blues. The Devil, people say, would run from Mr. Ford.

He killed a man in Tennessee when he was young, stabbing him in the neck with a switchblade after the man buried a knife in his back. "They gave me 10 years," he said. "Mama got a lawyer and got me out in two."

Once, when asked if he had killed anyone else, he replied, "Do I count the one I run over in my Pontiac?"   25

He was, in his wilder days—which have lasted pretty much all of his 79 years—a bar fighter and a moonshine drinker. "I have fathered 26 living children," he said. "I have married five times, and I have divorced from all of them."

Then, quick as he can change chords, his voice slipped from bragging to blues.

"There was a woman I would have married, if she had lived," he said. "She was a big, fine-looking woman, but she died in my arms. Four years ago. Best woman I ever had. I loved her."

She was married to another man, so Mr. Ford—what people here would call her back-door man—was not welcome at her funeral. "I just stood on the road and watched," he said.

He thought about that a bit, then told a young man, a   30 drummer who was napping on his couch, to "go out there behind the seat of that truck and get me that bottle of Jack."

His big hands danced across the strings. "I get to drinking," he said, "and I'm a bad man."

> Sent to the doctor
> Shot full of holes
> Nurse cried,
> "Save his soul."
> I'm a back-door man
> I'm a back-door man
> What the mens don't know
> The little girls understand.

BEYOND BLUES

If T-Model Ford is a character from one of his songs, CeDell
Davis is the sadness not even the blues can describe.

When he was a little boy, a man working in a pea patch
near his house in Helena, Arkansas, dropped a harmonica,
and Mr. Davis found it in the weeds.

35   "I liked the sound," he said. He unwrapped wire from a
broom handle and stretched it on a stick to make a crude guitar. He learned to play a real guitar, a big Gibson.

Then the polio twisted him. "They said I would die, and
when I didn't, they said I could never care for myself."

He figured a way to steady his guitar in his lap, above his
useless legs, wedged a butter knife between his thumb and
fingers that were stiff and clumsy; and, over time, learned to
strum with one hand and pinch the strings with the knife in a
way that makes the instrument seem to cry, as if alive.

He traveled the world, in fame and pain. He played in New
York to packed houses, and in St. Louis, where he was tram-
pled by a panicked crowd during a police raid. The worse of
his bad legs was shattered.

Like Mr. Jones and Mr. Ford, he made some money, squan-
dered it, got cheated out of some, and now lives in a small
house that from the outside gives no sign a legend is inside.

40   But some days he gets out his guitar, "Bessie, named for a
pretty, light-skinned woman I used to know," and music blows
through the screen doors and sweeps the sadness away.

> If you like fat women
> Come to Pine Bluff, Arkansas
> You know they got more fat women
> Than any place you ever saw.

DUCKING AT SYLVESTER'S

To Paul Jones, the blues will always smell like teacakes. It was
what his mother baked as she sang. His daddy was a guitar
man. By the time he was 8, he knew his destiny.

"The Belzoni police stopped me and my daddy one time,
but they just said, 'Hey, get that boy out and let him play,' and

they took me to the station and I played, and they threw quarters in the hole in my guitar."

He played the harsh clubs of the Delta, like Sylvester's, where his sister was shot by accident by a jealous woman, where a man fired a shotgun at him as he played. The closest he came to dying was about 2 a.m., coming back from Oxford, Mississippi, when his 1974 Chevrolet broke down. It was 17 degrees, and he almost froze.

Though he played all his life, it was welding that paid the bills. He would like to pass his music on, "but I got five kids, and nary a one of them plays."

Ms. Smith of the Blues Museum in Clarksdale said the 45
music that was once such a part of daily life here must now be kept alive by programs like the one in her museum, which is teaching blues to about 40 students.

Venessia Young, a 17-year-old high school senior who plays wicked guitar, is one of them. Her classmates refuse to listen to blues.

But when she hears it, she hears something Paul Jones and CeDell Davis and T-Model Ford hear.

"I'm going to attend Mississippi State next year, and they want me to play in a jazz group," she said.

"But that music, I just don't feel it."

Dance: Enriching Lives by Relearning African Culture
VALERIE GLADSTONE

Valerie Gladstone is a writer for *The Nation* and a contributing editor at *Dance* magazine. She is the co-author of *Balanchine's Mozartiana: The Making of a Masterpiece*.

My Thoughts in Writing

1. Why was the Dance Africa festival established and how does it help the community maintain its heritage? What particular traditions are highlighted at the festival?

2. Throughout the essay Gladstone highlights the role of African dance in the life of the community. What role does dance play and what specific purposes does it serve?

3. How are the dance groups Forces of Nature and Sabar Ak Ru Afriq similar? How do they differ? How does their work speak to the value and vitality of tradition?

———————— ✦ ————————

It was unusually busy on West 127th Street in Harlem one warm afternoon last month as a spirited procession of children and adults headed to the Dempsey Multiservice Center. Every Sunday, Obara Wali Rahman Ndiaye, 54, and his wife, Andara Rahman Ndiaye, 41, teach African dance classes there and rehearse their 35-member company, Sabar Ak Ru Afriq (Drum and Spirit of Africa, in the Senegalese language Wolof). They were getting ready for the popular Dance Africa festival, coming to the Brooklyn Academy of Music on Friday and running through next Sunday.

In 1977, the choreographer and educator Chuck Davis established the event to give African-Americans an opportunity to see top-flight African and African-influenced dance companies. "We need reminders of our history," he said recently. "It adds meaning to our lives."

This year, along with Sabar Ak Ru Afriq, Dance Africa will present Forces of Nature, a New York-based dance company, and in its first American appearance, the Ndere Troupe of Uganda. The theme is "Rhythms From the Circle of Life." Thirty youngsters from the BAM/Restoration Dance Africa Ensemble, a local community group, will perform dances taught them by the Ndere Troupe. Also scheduled are an art show, film screenings and an African dance party. The Dance Africa Bazaar, featuring foods, clothing, art and handicrafts, will be set up in a parking lot near BAM.

5   Even without the Dempsey Center's security guard telling a visitor where to find Mr. and Mrs. Rahman Ndiaye, the sounds of drums and children's laughter lead one to the big, sparkling gym, which, with basketball courts and all, becomes their dance

studio every week. Like most dance companies, Sabar Ak Ru Afriq and Forces of Nature make do with limited funds, which means dancers support themselves with other jobs. But while one would never see children at most dance rehearsals, they are inevitably around when these troupes rehearse, to relieve the parents of finding babysitters. It appears to make everyone pretty happy, and it creates an unusually homey atmosphere.

As an adult session ended, a woman in a long flowered skirt walked slowly toward her belongings. "It's not just my feet that hurt," she said, wincing, "everything hurts." Her son giggled, having gone through the same exertions an hour before.

After class, Mr. Rahman Ndiaye, gray haired and bearded, took a break in his small, drum-filled office in the back of the gym. "When I was coming up in New York, African drumming only existed in community centers," he said. "After the National Ballet of Senegal performed here in 1973, I got close with some of the people in the company. What attracted me was Sabar, a Senegalese style of dancing and drumming. It's rich in artistic value and relates to African-American styles of movement."

Wearing a purple and violet African dress, Mrs. Rahman Ndiaye joined him, her long hair pulled back by a matching scarf. Their backgrounds mesh well: he came from jazz; she studied modern and folkloric dance after moving here as a child from Carriacou, Grenada. To learn African dance firsthand, they traveled to Senegal and in New York studied with a Senegalese teacher, Adja Ma'am Fatou Seck, who died in 1997. Since founding the company in 1980, they have developed their own system of working: He suggests the themes, she choreographs and performs, and in the final stages they edit pieces together.

"My choreography derives from Senegalese styles," she said. "Essentially, it's celebratory and makes rigorous use of the torso, hips and arms."

Their daughter, Mariama, knocked on the door, reminding 10 them it was time to start. Their daughters, Mariama, 17, and Fatouseck, 8, and their sons, Latir, 20, and Konate, 14, grew up in the company. For the last couple of years, Mr. Rahman Ndiaye has been caring for a sick family member, and with Mrs. Rahman Ndiaye holding a full-time position as a supervisor at the Greenwood Job Center in Brooklyn, plus finishing graduate school, they have had to limit their performance schedule. So it is with particular zeal that they gear up for "Revival," a premiere for Dance Africa.

At Mr. Rahman Ndiaye's signal, the 15 dancers formed two diagonals and started across the room in a rolling gait, their voices rising in a gentle melody. The drumming intensified, and Mrs. Rahman Ndiaye separated herself from the group and implored another dancer to join her. "The piece comes out of folklore," Mr. Rahman Ndiaye said, watching them carefully. "After a spirit coaxes the girl into womanhood, she must be taught to take care of herself. We need to know these stories. When we relearn our culture, we restore our souls."

In the same vein but with a different aesthetic, the choreographer and musician Abdel R. Salaam, 50, creates dances for Forces of Nature. Later that week, he rehearsed one evening in the crypt of the Cathedral of St. John the Divine on the Upper West Side, his company's base since 1984. His subterranean headquarters are formidable. Cavernous, with a soaring vaulted ceiling, they consist of his office, handsomely decorated with African sculpture, and a good-size rehearsal space framed by towering columns. "When I started the company, some of my dancers who practiced African religions got upset when they learned that a couple of bishops were buried down here," said Mr. Salaam, a hefty man dressed entirely in black from his skull cap to his billowing trousers. "It seemed blasphemous to them to literally dance on their graves. So I had a priest come in and bless the space. That reassured them."

A New Yorker, Mr. Salaam first studied modern dance at Lehman College in the Bronx, rounding out his training with various jazz techniques. In 1970, he joined Mr. Davis's company, leaving to form his own group in 1981. "Chuck taught me that a dance should have a message," he said, "and that a choreographer should be socio-politically aware."

Mr. Salaam's dances, often prompted by African and American Indian culture, are far from polemical, however. After duplicating African dances for years, he began creating his own hybrid, impelled by a friendly suggestion. "Chuck and I were working with a master drummer from Ballet Afrique in the mid-80's," he recalled, "and when we finished one of our dances, he asked: 'But what's your story? It's important to tell your own story.'"

That night fewer than half of his 22 members made the   15 rehearsal. Naeemah Brown, a police officer, arrived late with apologies. She quickly got out of her uniform and into a yellow African skirt and white T-shirt. The dancers began with "Club Legacy," set to a score by Michael Wimberly. "The movement is a mix of modern, house, hip-hop and African," Mr. Salaam said. "There's a D.J. and scratching rhythms. A lot of the foundation of club music is African. I like the ride of it."

Moving like quicksilver, the dancers formed elaborate patterns and for several minutes all went well. Then suddenly, the whole thing got away from them. They burst out laughing.

"Abdel's work is so complex technically and mentally," his longtime rehearsal director, Laniece Mobley, said, with an eye on her 11-month-old daughter, Amina, contentedly bouncing in her stroller, "that when dancers from other companies first join, it takes them months to catch on."

Next, they tackled a section of "Terrestrial Wombs," a moving retelling of the story of creation. On its premiere in 1997, Jennifer Dunning of The New York Times called it "beautiful-looking and thought-provoking." Standing between the drummers Kojo Christopher and Randal Alston, Mr. Salaam set the tone on his drums, mixing Nigerian and Malian tempos with blazing results. "The bishops buried down here," he said, hands flying, "must love this."

A Feast of Fiddling (with Views)
Dirk Van Susteren

Dirk Van Susteren has written for *The New York Times* and is the Sunday Magazine editor for *The Barre Montpelier Times Argus*.

My Thoughts in Writing

1. According to the author, what event led to the resurgence of Cape Breton's "beloved music tradition"? What is the state of the tradition today?
2. Why is it important to the people of Cape Breton that their tradition live on? What tactics have they developed to maintain and celebrate their tradition? When it comes to carrying the tradition on, what essential element have they engaged and how? What other traditions have the people of Cape Breton maintained as a result of their dedication to their musical heritage?
3. Van Susteren uses vivid sensory detail and maintains a lively pace as he brings the music and people of Cape Breton to life. Locate places in the essay where Van Susteren's writing style is particularly effective. How does his writing style reflect his subject matter and theme?

———————— ✦ ————————

THIRTY years ago the Canadian Broadcasting Corporation televised a documentary, "The Vanishing Cape Breton Fiddler," that struck a jarring note on that island off the Nova Scotia mainland. It warned that Cape Breton's beloved music tradition was in trouble: The younger generation seemed to prefer the hard beat of modern rock to the sophisticated melodies of its Scottish forebears. Like all art forms, Celtic music needed young blood to survive.

Fortunately, the program was heard more as a bugle call than a dirge by Cape Bretoners who cared most about the music. In kitchen rackets (house parties) and at ceilidhs (Gaelic for gatherings) in community halls across the island, residents began promoting fiddle-playing as never before. Music lessons were offered and festivals were held.

And two years later, in an event now considered a benchmark in the Cape Breton music tradition, 100 fiddlers took to an outdoor stage at St. Mary of the Angels Church in the small town of Glendale to prove that island fiddling was alive and well. As thousands cheered, the Rev. John Angus Rankin, an

organizer of the event and a hero in the revival, declared tri-
umphantly that the documentary had been dead wrong.

Echoes of that grand Glendale event are now heard at the
Celtic Colors International Festival, an annual October series
of concerts that presents the music in a most varied and concentrated form. The nine-day festival is a celebration of the
music that Scottish immigrants brought to the island—now
connected by a causeway to the mainland—two centuries ago.
The festival, which will be held Oct. 5 to 13 this year, coincides
with the foliage season, when the red maple, birch and cherry
trees that dot the fir-covered hillsides are at their fiery best. As
many as five concerts are held in different communities across
the island each night; the festival also offers daytime lectures
and workshops on such subjects as Gaelic folklore, weaving
and the Highland pipes.

Traditional Cape Breton fiddle tunes, lively and melodi-   5
ous, and often played with keyboard accompaniment, are the
festival's mainstay. But there are also plenty of accordions,
pipes and drums—not to mention electronic amplification—
that add rock flavors to the Celtic mix. Many performers come
from Scotland, Ireland and Brittany, and about half of the
8,000 visitors come from off the island, drawn to the music by
international performances of such renowned Cape Breton
musicians as the Rankins, Natalie MacMaster, Buddy Mac-
Master and Ashley MacIsaac. These musicians grew up in the
Mabou region, heart of Cape Breton fiddling, where I began a
five-day immersion into Celtic music last fall.

Over the course of the visit, I heard foreign artists, including Dougie MacLean of Scotland, a songwriter, guitarist and
singer; Ishbel MacAskill of Scotland, a Gaelic vocalist; Filska,
a red-hot band from the Shetlands; and Daimh, a band of
young men from Ireland, California, Scotland and Cape Breton, whose varied national origins demonstrate how Celtic
music is cross-pollinating. Among the island's own performers
I heard J. P. Cormier and Dave MacIsaac, guitarists and fiddlers; Howie MacDonald, Sandy MacIntyre and Buddy Mac-
Master, all fiddlers; Paul MacNeil, a bagpiper; and Tracey
Dares MacNeil, a pianist. Members of the Barra MacNeils, a

spirited family group and one of Cape Breton's favorites, seemed to be everywhere during the festival.

Visitors can join the fun on any day in any town for a per-concert cost ranging from $8 to $50 in United States currency, at $1.55 (Canadian) to the U.S. dollar (many of the workshops and lectures, however, are free). The venues can be 40, 70 or 100 miles apart, so a good set of wheels and a plan for overnight accommodations are needed. But there are plenty of inns and bed-and-breakfasts, and camping also is an option. The miles pile up, but the tedium is diminished by the ocean, mountain and farmland views along winding country roads.

The festival's unofficial headquarters is the Gaelic College of Celtic Arts and Crafts on St. Anns Bay, about an hour north-east of Mabou. It is worth a stop. The tiny, rustic college offers instruction during the year in music, literature and language of the Gael. But the college's lure for Celtic Colors visitors are the concerts and all-night ceilidhs (pronounced KAY-lees) on its campus and a gift shop with musical instruments, tartan blankets, kilts, Gaelic books, and, of course, tapes and CD's.

After a daytime stop at the college, I drove on a cool and blustery evening to the new Dalbrae Academy in Mabou, near the western coast, for a concert that proved a showcase of homegrown talent. Among the performers were the local teenage fiddlers and step dancers Dawn and Margie Beaton, sisters who come from a long line of Cape Breton musicians. Another face familiar to locals was that of the piper Angus MacKenzie, a Mabou native and a member of the band Daimh. MacKenzie, a tall redhead, received good wishes and a kiss before stepping to the stage with the three other members in his band. With fiddles, bodhran (an Irish drum) and man-dola (somewhat like a mandolin), the young men played a few plaintive tunes. Then they began the jigs, strathspeys and reels that set hundreds of feet tapping.

10   There were a few glitches. Because the auditorium was still under construction, the concert was in the gym. Unfortu-nately, that meant fiddle and piano notes were bouncing off walls meant for errant basketballs, creating some auditory confusion. And twice during performances, a balky fire alarm sounded, interrupting the music. The blaring noise

prompted a Daimh member to joke: "Can we smoke now?" But the audience remained unfazed; on with the music, it seemed to say.

Two nights later, at the Gaelic College, young musicians were again featured. They were the youth members of the Cape Breton Fiddlers Association, an organization formed shortly after the broadcast of "The Vanishing Cape Breton Fiddler." In the college's main hall, a stone building with clan tartans draping the walls, dozens of youngsters from the 500-member association played traditional fiddle music together; others then played solos, or step danced as Sheumas MacNeil of the Barra MacNeils played keyboard.

But it wasn't entirely kids' night. Gerry Deveau, 66, of Chéticamp, a town settled by French immigrants, wowed the audience with his spoon playing as Kyle MacNeil, brother of Sheumas, performed furiously on the fiddle. Deveau—spoons clicking on knees, thighs, shoulders—was a study in motion.

The regular concert ended at 10:30, when the night owls in the audience stepped outside for fresh air, only to line up again at 11 for the ceilidh. Four dollars and they were back in. A few more bucks bought beer and pizza.

With backs to a large, blazing fireplace, they listened, feet tapping, as musicians cut loose on stage. These after-hours bashes, lasting past sunup, seemed to draw a younger, hipper and more international crowd. No one looked as if he had to work that very morning. Twenty-somethings traded e-mail addresses. A San Diego woman asked Deveau to consider trading his set of spoons for her set of "bones"—clappers used for keeping time to the music.

The ceilidh began with the Barra MacNeils; joining Kyle and Sheumas were their sister, Lucy, playing bodhran, and their brother Stewart, on the flute and the accordion. Around 1 a.m. the band Slàinte Mhath (pronounced Slawn-cha-VAH), a group with two more MacNeil siblings, took the stage. They apologized for what was expected to be an abbreviated performance—they were leaving for Ontario later that day—then went on to play until nearly 3 a.m. The fiddling virtuoso Kendra MacGillivray was stepping to the stage when, exhausted, I called it a morning.

15

Nights blend too quickly into days, and newcomers to Cape Breton must exert some personal discipline if touring is to be done. Among the most popular daytime attractions are the Miners' Museum in Glace Bay; the Fortress of Louisbourg, a reconstruction of the French 18th century outpost; and the famous 190-mile Cabot Trail. This mountainous road winds around the island's northeastern corner, affording views of crashing surf and, in autumn, dazzling forest colors. Determined tourists may want to take the road to Cape Breton Highlands National Park, but exploring this remote coastal preserve, where one might see both whales and moose, will cut deeply into music time.

A less time-consuming side trip more in keeping with the festival's theme would be a visit to the Highland Village Museum in Iona. Set on 40 acres, it features various buildings— homes, a barn, a general store and a blacksmith shop—used by Scottish immigrants and moved to the site. On a cool day, with the scent of wood smoke and lanolin in the air, visitors walked the paths between the structures and learned about island life in the 19th century from docents in period costumes. Members of the staff weaved and did farm chores—reminders that immigrant life was hard in the New World despite the fiddles.

I attended a festival workshop on immigration patterns and island architecture at the library in Sydney and heard a talk on Celtic storytelling there at the University College of Cape Breton. And at the St. Mary parish center in Glendale, near the site of Father Rankin's original concert, I attended a step-dancing workshop and eavesdropped on bagpiping lessons.

The workshop attracted some two dozen people, but about half of them were young Cape Bretoners who wanted to hone existing skills. An adult parishioner said that step dancing and fiddling traditions are again becoming ingrained in the younger generation. Among teenagers, he said, fiddle cases now carry the cachet of hockey bags.

20   The festival ended with a bang in Baddeck, the popular tourist town on Bras d'Or Lake. Music fans had two choices on the final night: The "Kitchen Ceilidh" at the high school, featuring the Barra MacNeils and other festival favorites; and "The World's Biggest Square Dance" at the civic center. I

picked the latter, because Buddy MacMaster, 75, was performing. He is one of the island's most beloved and talented fiddlers and has done as much, or more, as anyone to keep the tradition alive. More than 1,000 people attended. Tables were arranged for beer drinkers, bleachers for wallflowers, and the floor for serious dancers.

The fingers of Tracey Dares MacNeil (not of the Barra MacNeils) flashed across the keyboard as her husband, Paul, took charge with the bagpipes; and Jenna Reid of Filska, lithe and leather-skirted, rocked the house with her electric fiddling.

There was square dancing, to be sure, but as always, just as much vigorous foot tapping to the lovely, speedy melodies. And in the wee hours, during the finale, things became most frenetic. With keyboards, guitars and pipes playing, eight fiddlers, taking cues from MacMaster and Sandy MacIntyre, another old-time Cape Breton fiddler, played a medley of familiar island tunes. A few members of the audience climbed the stage to step dance. There was jitterbugging and improvisational dance—even a version of the hora.

It was impossible to stand still, or believe for a moment the future of this music was ever in doubt.

A Heritage in Clay and Copper
Jonathan Kandell

Jonathan Kandell, a freelance writer based in New York, grew up in Mexico City in the 1950s. He is the author of *La Capital: The Biography of Mexico City* (1988).

My Thoughts in Writing

1. In the first line of his essay, Kandell writes that his "childhood memories of Mexico during the 1950's are wrapped in rebozos." How does this statement relate to Kandell's

search through provincial Mexico for the keepers of its cultural heritage? What does he find on his journey?

2. Why, according to the artisans in the essay, do the young people refuse to engage in traditional crafting? What is the result of this turning away from tradition?

3. How does Kandell feel about the artisans he encounters? What does he learn from them about the role of tradition in life? Use specific words and phrases from the text to illustrate your answer.

———————— ✦ ————————

My childhood memories of Mexico during the 1950's are wrapped in rebozos: young women on their way to parties, resplendent in shawls woven from fine cotton dipped in natural dyes; a mother and infant blanketed and tethered by a swath of plain gray or brown.

Moroleón, a prosperous city in the central Mexican state of Guanajuato, was once famous as home of the finest rebozo weavers. Here, Taller La Mexicana is one of the last workshops in the country to produce rebozos the traditional way, on creaking, foot-powered wooden looms. The 13 weavers are all in late middle age. I watched the oldest as he wove a shawl of black-and-white tie-dyed, silky cotton that will retail for about $100.

His right hand plied a stick that raised and lowered the threads, and the fingers of his left hand deftly guided new strands through the fabric in a motion that resembled the plucking of a harp. Meanwhile, his feet pedaled away, moving the loom up, down and sideways. His face was utterly serene, as if he was in a trance, heedless of the constant clickety-clack. In a day, he finishes up to five rebozos.

"Young people won't put up with this work," said Luis Guzmán López, the 73-year-old owner of Taller La Mexicana, started by his ancestors six generations ago. Young Mexicans aren't buying good rebozos, either. Moroleón, a manufacturing center for international clothing concerns, is a fashion-conscious place, but the women wear American and European designs, said Mr. Guzmán, who doubts that his business will outlive him. "They think rebozos are for poor Indians. They're turning their backs on a cultural heritage."

Over the last several years, I have spent vacations (most   5
recently in October) traveling through provincial Mexico
searching for the keepers of this cultural heritage—the aging
master weavers, ceramists, carvers and metalworkers. I have
met some of Mexico's finest artisans in the adjoining states of
Michoacán and Guanajuato, a region known for crafts that
meld Indian traditions and colonial Spanish techniques. To
view and buy their works, a visitor must usually seek them out
at their homes. I started out with certain advantages, including fluent Spanish and a thorough knowledge of the terrain.
But most travelers can do as well by hiring a car and English-
speaking driver-guide through hotels in Morelia and Guanajuato, the capitals of Michoacán and Guanajuato.

I began with a drive from Morelia 70 miles west to the
artisanal town of Uruapan. The arid terrain gave way to a ver-
dant, river-drained landscape of cornfields and banana plantations. Uruapán itself was a visual disappointment—an over-
grown service center for nearby farms that has devoured more
picturesque villages on its outskirts.

The first master artisan on my list was 88-year-old Fran-
cisca Tulais Urbina, one of the last practitioners of macre
(MAH-kray), a pre-Hispanic wood lacquering technique that
achieves a warmer, less glossy surface than Asian methods. A
few years earlier I had seen her platters and bowls at an artisan fair in Mexico City. But finding Ms. Tulais wasn't easy. I
had only her photograph (clipped from a magazine) and the
name of her street. When I asked neighbors about her, they
shrugged, until finally, an elderly woman looked at the picture
and exclaimed: "Ay, that's Panchita the milkmaid!"

Ms. Tulais—Panchita—had indeed tended cows for much
of her life. I found her in the patio of her house, under a rubber tree, spreading paint with her fingers over a wooden bowl
she had carved. An old vacuum-tube radio blared a plaintive
ranchera—Mexican country music—by Pedro Infante, a favorite from my childhood days.

Ms. Tulais learned her art from her grandmother, but
practiced it only at the end of the day after delivering milk.
Now at last she sells enough objects to devote herself full time
to macre. It takes her almost a month to complete a piece—

though she works on as many as four at a time, since they require several layers of lacquer and paint that must be allowed to dry before each application. She uses only local softwood species and mineral dyes made of materials collected from nearby riverbanks.

10   Ms. Tulais, who never married, is hoping that two nieces will take up her work. "Younger people find this work too dirty," she said. "They look at my fingernails and say, 'How disgusting!'" Some of her pieces were on display in a tiled corridor nearby: lacquered trays, jewel boxes and bowls with bird and flower designs. The smaller objects cost as little as $20. For $150, I bought a huge platter with mangoes and papayas etched on a cobalt blue background.

Another great artisan in his 80's, Victoriano Salgado Morales, a maker of wooden masks, lives only 10 blocks away. Uruapan was once famous for its masks, which are used by dancers in festivals, and Mr. Salgado is one of the last masters of the art. Rail-thin and wearing denim overalls, he beckoned me onto the terrace where he does his carving and painting behind his adobe-walled house.

He was working on a mask of a wrinkled face with a slightly sinister smile, part of a set for la danza de los viejitos (the dance of the old folk) to be held in a nearby village. As he sandpapered a mask, he explained how he became an artisan.

"My family had always been day laborers, completely landless, the poorest of the poor," he told me. "When I was a boy, the only possible escape seemed to be mask-making." But the dozen mask-makers in his village all guarded their craft zealously, so Mr. Salgado had to learn on his own. He soon became known as an innovator. "People thought I had more imagination than the others because I was inspired by faces from old cartoon magazines," he says. Nowadays his clients include collectors throughout Mexico who pay $50 to $60 for a mask.

The last of the trio of Uruapan master artisans I visited was Marta Morales Naranjo, inventor of her own genre—miniature dolls, made of cloth and wire, representing folklore figures. Ms. Morales, who is 76, lives with her aunt, Carmen, in a rambling house on a hill sloping up from a river. She shapes the armature of the six-to-eight-inch dolls and sews their costumes on, while her 92-year-old aunt does the embroidering. "Her eyesight is a lot better than mine," said Ms. Morales, peering through thick bifocals.

The living room floor, where she receives her collectors, is   15
cluttered with boxes of 50-year-old silk in every imaginable hue. "I've bought enough for the rest of my life because they don't make material of this quality anymore," she said. On shelves along the walls are her figurines of fishmongers, tortilla makers, bird sellers—a hundred different street peddlers in all. Each doll sells for about $50.

On the way back to Morelia, I veered south at Pátzcuaro for 10 miles to Santa Clara del Cobre. Celebrated for its copper artisans, this is a lovely town of cobblestone side streets and whitewashed adobe houses with dark-wood balconies and red-tiled roofs. A couple of blocks behind the main church, I found the home of Jesús Pérez Ornelas, 76. In his roofed but open-sided workshop, he and two sons were melting a nest of copper wire in a forge fired by pine charcoal.

The copper emerged in lumpy plates and was dipped into cold water that sizzled and steamed angrily. With giant iron pincers the old man held the copper plate on a tree stump shaped into an enormous block of wood, while his sons wielded sledgehammers to pound the copper flat.

Mr. Pérez wrapped the copper over a wax mold, and began to hammer the metal into its ultimate shape—an oval-mouthed vessel with a hawk's head at each end. He then used a small hammer and pick to etch the surface with geometric and animal patterns.

The idea for those patterns came from a visit 40 years ago to the National Museum of Anthropology in Mexico City where he saw pre-Columbian ceramics for the first time. "I wanted to reproduce in copper the same designs—well, maybe not the same, but similar ones," said Mr. Pérez, who learned his craft from an uncle. Most of his vessels sell for $300 to $500.

20   A few days later I headed north from Morelia to the state of Guanajuato. Moroleón, the former rebozo center, is a mere 30 miles away. The city of Guanajuato, my ultimate destination, is 90 miles farther.

Guanajuato is built on a mountain that once held the world's richest silver deposits, and its winding, cobblestone streets are as steeply angled as ski slopes. An underground warren of tunnels helps relieve congestion on the surface, but left me hopelessly lost. After almost an hour of wasted driving, I found the house of Gorky González, one of Mexico's most celebrated master artisans.

His finely glazed pottery pieces—from a single $11 cup to a waist-high urn retailing at $1,500—are favored by the country's leading architects and interior designers. Hidden behind a towering wall, his house and studio are a wondrous refuge from urban sprawl and clatter.

Gorky, as everybody calls him, got his name because his father, a left-wing intellectual, adored the Russian writer Maxim Gorky. As a young man, Gorky González painted and did sculpture, until one day, rummaging through his father's antiques shop, he found pottery made with a double-glaze technique imported from Mediterranean Europe and known as majolica. The technique had been abandoned in Mexico in the 1820's after independence from Spain because it was identified with the colonial elite.

But Gorky was so drawn to majolica that he resolved to become a ceramist. "The notion of rescuing a forgotten craft—especially one so beautiful—was impossible to resist," said Gorky, whose unlined face and thick, black hair and mustache belie his 62 years.

25   Nowadays he has several assistants reproducing his designs while he concentrates on unique pieces. They work with clay extracted from the nearby Sierra de Santa Rosa, a source for Indian ceramists long before the arrival of the Spaniards in the 1500's. Shaped on potter's wheels and dried in adobe-walled storerooms, the pieces are decorated with plant, animal or folkloric figures in subtle blue, green, yellow and beige hues, then baked in modern electric ovens. A tin oxide enamel

glaze is applied, and the works are baked again, this time at much higher temperatures. Samples of the pieces—vases, planters, dinner sets—are on display in a showroom.

Gorky's second son (also named Gorky), who apprenticed with his father and hopes to succeed him as master artisan someday, is responsible for the high-tech ovens, Internet communications and express shipping. Admittedly, it's not an operation that evokes the rebozo-garbed nostalgia of my childhood. But I feel a lot more hopeful about Mexico's cultural heritage knowing that a lost art can thrive again using modern methods.

Folklife in Contemporary Multicultural Society

RICHARD KURIN

Richard Kurin, born 1950, is the director of the Center for Folklife Programs and Cultural Heritage, in Washington D.C. He wrote the essay from which the following excerpts are taken in an effort to explain to visitors at the 1990 Festival of American Folklife the symbolic cultural significance of folklife.

My Thoughts in Writing

1. How does Kurin help refine our understanding of folklife in the first three paragraphs of his essay? What does he assert folklife is? What does he tell us it is not? According to Kurin, what happens when we view folklife incorrectly, as a "theatrical recreation of the past"?
2. Why, in Kurin's view, do we have a tendency to devalue folklife? What evidence does he give to prove there has been a delegitimization of "grass-roots, peoples' culture," a move away from traditional loyalties, a devaluing of the past in order to overcome it?
3. How does Kurin feel about a multicultural society? What are our responsibilities to that society? What is the role of

the Festival of American Folklife in "an increasingly diverse and multicultural society"? What does that role entail, and how, according to Kurin, might it be achieved?

——————— ✦ ———————

Expressive, grass-roots culture, or folklife, is lived by all of us as members of ethnic, religious, tribal, familial or occupational groups. It is the way we represent our values in stories, songs, rituals, crafts and cooking. Whether the legacy of past generations or a recent innovation, folklife is traditionalized by its practitioners; it becomes a marker of community or group identity. Folklife is a way that people say, "This is who and how we are."

Folklife is as contemporary as it is historical: it is the languages and dialects we speak, the clothes we wear and the other ways in which we express ourselves. It is gospel music performed by African American choirs, Anglo-American foodways, stories taxicab drivers tell, group dances done at Jewish weddings, whistle signals of Salvadoran men, Missouri fiddling sessions and the practical knowledge farmers have of weather; it is Italians playing *bocce*, Vietnamese curing by rubbing, Puerto Ricans playing the *plena*, Ojibway Indians harvesting wild rice, Pakistanis eating *dal* and *chapati*. While implicating the past, these traditions are as *contemporary* in their expressivity and function as abstract painting, computer synthesized music and microwavable food. Traditional Virgin Islands scratch band music and calypso singing, *kallaloo* cooking and mask making are contemporary with top 40 hits, fast food and the tourist industry. In Senegal, saying *namaz*, singing praise songs, dancing the *sabar*, participating in *lambe* wrestling, and practicing metal smithing, cloth dying and hair braiding are part of contemporary lives.

Folklife is often and wrongfully associated in the popular mind with incomprehensible song and stilted dance, doll-like performance costumes, and antiquated, naive arts and crafts. Despite the advertising label, folklife is not a large group of choreographed, acrobatic, finely tailored youth prancing to glorious orchestral music in romanticized and theatrically inspired visions of peasant life. Nor does folklife properly refer to historical re-enactments of bygone crafts or to other anachronistic performances in which individuals pretend to be others situated in a distant time and place. This tendency to think of folklife as theatrical recreation of the past disparages it, divorces it from its contemporary existence.

The devaluation of grass-roots, peoples' culture grows from a desire to see ourselves as "modern." This desire, as many social historians have noted, is rooted in the practices of the industrial revolution and their ideological consequences. Industrial manufacture—with its rationalization of production to maximize profit—meant relying on those applied sciences that fostered innovative technological development and giving primary legitimacy to systems of value based upon or well-suited to an economic calculus. In the 19th century, many older forms of knowledge, systems of values, technologies and skills that were not useful to factory manufacture, to American and European urban life, and to a growing class of professional scholars, were delegitimated.

An example of this is the official devaluation and delegiti-   5
mation of medical systems, such as the Greco-Roman-Arabic humoral system, or "Ionian Physics." This system of medicine practiced from the Mediterranean to south Asia had a rich pharmacoepia, an experimental tradition, colleges and training center, a long-lived, vibrant literature, and tens of thousands of trained physician practitioners serving both urban and rural communities. Yet it was devalued by British colonial officials. Because they held power, not a necessarily or demonstrably better science, they were able to decertify local practitioners and institutions. The result was that medical treatment by indigenous physicians was lost to many, particularly in rural areas. The relatively few locals trained in British medical schools either returned primarily to cities or stayed abroad. The denial of other, in this case, was also a denial of one's own history. Hippocrates himself, the fountain-head of Western medical practice, practiced the humoral system. Greco-Roman scholars developed the system's pharmacopeia and theory, which, preserved and expanded by Arab physicians, was still taught in European universities well into the 19th century.

Concurrent with the monopolistic assertion of singular, exclusive ways of knowing and forms of knowledge, European and American nations invested power in institutions that transcended traditional loyalties. Allegiance to family, clan, religious sect and tribe might be seen as primordial bases of nationhood, but they had to be ethically superseded for the state to function. This transformation was understood as a fundamental shift in the nature of society by seminal theorists of the late 19th century—from mechanical to organic forms of solidarity by Emile Durkheim, from community to association by Ferdinand Tonnies, from status to civil society by Lewis Henry Morgan, from feudalism to capitalism by Max Weber and Karl Marx. The success of this transformation can be seen in the permanency of its non-folk forms of organization—universities and school systems, judicial courts, parliaments and political parties, businesses and unions—which came to define particular fields of social action. Less formal types of organization—church, home, family, elders, neighborhood, club—receded in importance.

The success of American and European efforts to develop state institutions—and thereby to overcome the past by devaluing it—were mistakenly taken to justify the ethical superiority of colonizing powers over peoples of Africa, Asia, Oceania and South America. An ideology of social and cultural evolution postulated necessary correspondences among technological development, social organization and cultural achievement. In the view of late 19th century social science, technologically advanced peoples were better organized socially and superior culturally. Modernity was opposed to tradition and was associated with political power; it was thought to be characteristic of more sophisticated, higher class, adult-like culture, while tradition was associated with powerlessness and thought to be associated with a simpler, lower class, child-like culture. According to this ideology, the purpose of education, development and cultural policy was for the supposedly deficient, tradition-bound peoples (both foreign and domestic) to follow in the technological, social and cultural footsteps of the advanced and modern.

This view has always been and continues to be challenged. Technological "progress" does not mean "better" for everyone.

Technological superiority may indeed mean more efficient production. But it can also mean more efficient destruction. Witness our modern ability for nuclear annihilation. Witness the devastation and pollution of the environment with efficient forest cutting machines and powerful but toxic synthetic chemicals. Witness the breakup of social units, cultural forms and ethical values resulting in part from television, video and computer games. The comparative efficacy of social systems is difficult to measure. While modern states are often judged positively for their nuclear families, social and geographic mobility and diffuse systems of authority, these forms have a cost. High divorce and suicide rates, urban crime, drug problems, mid-life crises and alienation are in part the prices paid for the type of society we live in.

It is difficult if not impossible to say that one culture is   10
better than another. All cultures provide a system of symbols and meanings to their bearers, and in this function they are similar. All cultures encourage self-perpetuating, guiding values and forms of aesthetic expression. All cultures encode knowledge, although the ways in which they do so may differ. And when one set of cultural ideas replaces another it is usually a case of knowledge replacing knowledge, not ignorance.

The relationship between ethics, power and technology is also problematic. Progress on technical and social fronts has not been uniform, even in Europe and the United States. Wide discrepancies continue to exist in the accessibility of technological benefits and social opportunities. Within the U.S. and Europe and around the world, the point is easily made that political or coercive power is not necessarily associated with righteousness. Modern states have inflicted ethical horrors upon each other—the world wars, for example, do not bespeak of advanced and civilized values. Nor do institutions such as slavery, colonialism, concentration camps and apartheid visited on the so-called "less developed" or "inferior" speak well of ethical or cultural superiority, as Frederick Douglass, Mohandas Gandhi, Elie Wiesel, Martin Luther King, Jr., Lech Walesa and Desmond Tutu have clearly demonstrated.

According to some interpreters of culture, the world is becoming more homogeneous. The spread of mass, popular commercial culture with a discrete set of television programs and formats, fast food, top music hits, designer jeans and other fashions, and a standard repertoire of consumer goods seems to have engulfed the planet. Modern technology—from television and radio to videocassette recorders, communications satellites, modems and fax machines—has seemingly reduced distances between the earth's peoples. We can send our voices and images around the planet in a matter of seconds.

Many cultures, as Alan Lomax (1977) has ably noted, are in moral and aesthetic danger as a result of this globalization of American mass culture, and as a result of the continued valorization of elite forms of culture. The power and frequency with which mass culture penetrates everyday life can suggest to people that local, grass-roots culture is not valuable. Publicity attending the purchases of masterpieces for multimillion dollar sums can give people the feeling that their own creations are relatively worthless. Some people stop speaking their local language, discontinue their art, music, foodways and other cultural expressions in the belief that imitating either mass or elite forms of culture is a route to a better position in the society. Old time music, storytelling, traditional dance, and boatbuilding cease, as do traditional forms of mutual support; a culture begins to die.

Cultures need to be conserved. Just as we mourn biological species when they become endangered and die out, so too do we mourn cultures that die. For each culture represents scores of traditions built up, usually over many generations. Each culture provides a unique vision of the world and how to navigate through it. Cultures are best conserved when they are dynamic, alive, when each generation takes from the past, makes it their own, contributes to it and builds a future. Cultural change and dynamism are integral to culture. Cultures were not created years ago to persist forever in unchanging form. Cultures are continually recreated in daily life as it is lived by real people.

15   For this reason, as Breckenridge and Appadurai (1988) suggest, the world is increasingly becoming at once more cul-

turally heterogeneous as well as more homogeneous. New variations of being Indian, for example, arise from cultural flows occasioned by the immigrant experience, tourism and reverse immigration. A Hindu temple, housed in a historic building, is established in Flushing, New York; fast food restaurants featuring an Indian spiced menu are built in New Delhi. New contexts occasion creative applications of traditional forms. New culture unlike that previously in New York or New Delhi is created.

Technology aids this process. Cheap, easy to use tape recorders, video cameras and the like begin to democratize the power of media. Anyone can make a recording or a film, preserve and document their cultural creation and share it with others. A videocassette recorder can be used in India to view *Rocky V*, but it can also be used to view a home video of a Hindu wedding sent by relatives living in New York.

The main issue in a monocultural society—whether relatively small and homogeneous or large and totalitarian—is that of control. Who has the power and authority to make culture, to promulgate it and have people accept it? Historically, in colonial situations, the colonizers have tended to dictate cultural choices and definitions of public and state culture. Those colonized accept in general terms the culture, language, garb, or religion of the powerful, and then continue their own ways in various forms of resistance. In this sense, those colonized, subjugated or out of power are often more multicultural than those in power—for it is they that are forced to learn two languages, to dress up and down, to participate in the "mainstream" as well as in their own culture. Individuals from the disempowered learn to be successful in both cultures by code switching—playing a role, speaking and acting one way with the out-group, another way with one's own people.

Increasing cultural homogeneity and heterogeneity calls for increased ability to participate in a variety of cultures—national, religious, occupational, tribal, ethnic and familial—on a daily basis. Code switching and compartmentalization are part of everyday life. For example, mainstream forms of language use, comportment and dress may be used in school or at work during the day, but may be replaced by a different dialect and style back home in the evening. Religious culture and occupational culture may be compartmentalized by an anthropology professor who teaches evolution during the week and Genesis at Sunday school. As our identities are increasingly multiple—as mothers, as workers, as household heads, for example—and as these identities are continually brought into juxtaposition, people will with greater awareness participate in and draw upon a multiplicity of cultures. Most Americans already eat foods from a variety of culinary traditions—though our palates are generally more multicultural than our minds. And in daily life we are liable to use a variety of languages—including not only "natural" languages but also those of word processing, mathematics and technical fields. One-dimensional views of ourselves and others as being members of either this culture or that culture will seem increasingly simplistic, irrelevant and unimaginative. Individual management of a multiplicity of roles and the cultural forms associated with them will offer new creative potentials for personality development, as well as, no doubt, new difficulties.

Socially, multiculturalism is a fact of life in many communities. Increasingly, formal institutions must respond to the consequences of a multicultural society. Educational and research organizations will have to facilitate skill in multiculturality. As geographic distance and boundaries become more easily traversed, we will simply have to achieve greater cross-cultural and intercultural fluency than we now possess. Monoculturalism, even amongst the most powerful, will be untenable. To be successful, Americans will have to learn about the Japanese, the Soviets, the Chinese, the Muslim world, and many others. And Americans will need greater self-knowledge if we are to deal with the increasing diversity of our neighborhoods and institutions. Cultural monologues will be out, dialogues or multilogues in, as we get used to the idea that there are different ways of knowing, feeling and expressing. As differences in perspective are institutionalized, our museums, schools, workplaces and other organizations will become richer, more multilayered and complex, informed by alternative, juxtaposed and newly synthesized varieties of aesthetic and conceptual orientations. The authority to speak and to know will be increasingly more widely distributed. Those who are traditionally studied, observed and written about may reverse roles. This is illustrated by the experience of Tony Seeger, a cultural anthropologist and curator of Smithsonian Folkways Records who did his fieldwork in the Brazilian rainforest among the Suya Indians. On his first trip in 1971, he recorded Suya songs and narrative in an effort to understand why the Suya sing. His book, *Why Suya Sing* (1987), is a masterful, scholarly attempt to interpret the significance of song in that culture. When Seeger returned to the field in 1980, the Suya had acquired tape recorders of their own. They were recording and listening to their own songs, as well as those from afar. As Suya themselves became cultural investigators, they recorded the banjo-picking Seeger and wanted to know why he also sings.

20

The role of the Festival of American Folklife in an increasingly diverse and multicultural society is to promote cultural equity, which is an equitable chance for all cultures to live and continue forward, to create and contribute to the larger pool of human intellectual, artistic and material accomplishment. The Festival fosters a general sense of appreciation for cultures so what they speak, know, feel and express may be understood. The Festival is a collaborative engagement that fosters dialogue or multilogue between community, self and others. Rather than encourage monocultural competitions, the Festival creates the time and space for cultural juxtapositions, where bearers of differing cultures can meet on neutral ground to experience the richness of making meaning, as well as the similarities that make them all human.

The Festival rests upon a moral code that affirms the cultural right to be human in diverse ways. People of different cultures must not continually find their culture devalued, their beliefs delegitimated and their kids being told they are not good enough. For official standards come and go very quickly and are often tied to a particular history and exercise of power.

Rather, we should respect the generations of knowledge, wisdom and skill that build a culture, and the excellences nurtured therein, so that, as Johnetta Cole, cultural anthropologist and president of Spelman College says, "We are for difference. For respecting difference. For allowing difference. Until difference doesn't make any more difference" (Cole 1990).

References

Cole, Johnetta. 1990. Quoted in *All Things Considered* news feature on Spelman College. National Public Radio. March 8.

Lomax, A. in Kurin, Richard. 1990. Folklife in Contemporary Multicultural Society *Festival of American Folklife Program Book* (Washington D.C.: Smithonian Institution and National Park Service, 1990).

The Idea of Ancestry

ETHERIDGE KNIGHT

One of seven children, Ethridge Knight was born on April 19, 1931 in Corinth, Mississippi. He joined the army in 1947, was discharged in 1957, and was arrested for robbery in 1960. Encouraged by members of the Black Arts movement, Knight began writing while serving his sentence in the Indiana State Prison. His poems reflect his experiences both in and out of prison and attest to the importance of family and community when defining the self.

My Thoughts in Writing

1. How does the speaker feel about his family members? How does he define his relationship to them? What do you think the last line of the poem has to do with the speaker's idea of family and his place within his own family unit?

2. Why does the speaker relate the story of his missing uncle? What do his uncle's actions and their effects on the

speaker's family have to do with the poem's overall message about the significance of family, of heritage, of ancestry?
3. Why does the speaker travel to Mississippi each year? What is significant about the trip described in the poem? How is the speaker affected by his time with his family members? What is unique about the activities in which they engage?

———————— ✦ ————————

1

Taped to the wall of my cell are 47 pictures: 47 black
faces: my father, mother, grandmothers (1 dead), grand
fathers (both dead), brothers, sisters, uncles, aunts,
cousins (1st & 2nd), nieces, and nephews. They stare
across the space at me sprawling on my bunk. I know   5
their dark eyes, they know mine. I know their style,
they know mine. I am all of them, they are all of me;
they are farmers, I am a thief, I am me, they are thee.

I have at one time or another been in love with my mother
1 grandmother, 2 sisters, 2 aunts (1 went to the asylum), 10
and 5 cousins. I am now in love with a 7 yr old niece
(she sends me letters written in large block print, and
her picture is the only one that smiles at me).

I have the same name as 1 grandfather, 3 cousins, 3
    nephews,
and 1 uncle. The uncle disappeared when he
    was 15, just took   15
off and caught a freight (they say). He's discussed
    each year
when the family has a reunion, he causes
    uneasiness in
the clan, he is an empty space. My father's mother,
    who is 93
and who keeps the Family Bible with everybody's birth dates
(and death dates) in it, always mentions him.
    There is no   20
place in her Bible for "whereabouts unknown."

2

Each fall the graves of my grandfathers call me, the
    brown
hills and red gullies of mississippi send out their
    electric
messages, galvanizing my genes. Last yr/like a
    salmon quitting
the cold ocean—leaping and bucking up his
    birthstream/I   25
hitchhiked my way from L.A. with 16 caps in my
    pocket and a
monkey on my back. And I almost kicked it with the
    kinfolks.

I walked barefooted in my grandmother's backyard/
    I smelled the old
land and the woods/I sipped cornwhiskey from
    fruit jars with the men /
I flirted with the women/I had a ball till the caps
    ran out   30
and my habit came down. That night I looked at my
    grandmother
and split/my guts were screaming for junk/
    but I was almost
contented/I had almost caught up with me.
The next day in Memphis I cracked a croaker's
    crib for a fix.

This yr there is a gray stone wall damming my
    stream, and when   35
the falling leaves stir my genes, I pace my cell or
    flop on my bunk
and stare at the 47 black faces across the space. I am all
    of them,
they are all of me, I am me, they are thee, and
    I have no sons
to float in the space between.   40

Legacies

NIKKI GIOVANNI

Nikki Giovanni was born in 1943 in Knoxville, Tennessee. She attended Fisk University and was a member of the Writer's Workshop and the Student Non-violent Coordinating Committee. In 1967, she became actively involved in the Black Arts movement and began creating poetry that reflected the revolutionary feel of the era. Her writing not only reflects her interest in writing and politics, but it is affected by her experiences as a single mother and her concern for family. She currently teaches at Virginia Polytechnic Institute.

My Thoughts in Writing

1. How does the grandmother feel about making rolls and teaching her granddaughter how to do it? How do you know? Which lines from the poem convey the grandmother's attitude?

2. The speaker tells us that the little girl didn't want to learn how to make rolls because "that would mean when the old one died she would be less / dependent on her spirit." What does it mean to be less dependent on someone's spirit? What does it mean in this particular instance? Analyze the other places of dialogue in the poem, and, in each instance of speech, determine what is not being said and why neither person "said what they meant."

3. Why do you think the poem shifts from third person to first person at the end? What is the effect and how does it relate to the poems overall message? Why might the speaker enter the poem so directly in the end?

———————— ✦ ————————

her grandmother called her from the playground
    "yes, ma'am"
    "i want chu to learn how to make rolls," said the old
woman proudly
but the little girl didn't want   5

to learn how because she knew
even if she couldn't say it that
that would mean when the old one died she would be less
dependent on her spirit so
she said   10
      "i don't want to know how to make no rolls"
with her lips poked out
and the old woman wiped her hands on
her apron saying "lord
    these children"
and neither of them ever   15
said what they meant
and i guess nobody ever does

Welcome to the Millennium
GERALD CELENTE

Gerald Celente is the director of the Trends Research Institute, in Rhinebeck, NY, and is known as a "trends forecaster." He is the author of the nationally syndicated column "Trends in the News" and the author of *Trends 2000: How to Prepare for Profit from the Changes of the 21st Century* (1997).

My Thoughts in Writing

1. Rather than a turning away from tradition and more traditional ways of life, what does Celente believe will occur in the coming century? What proof of his viewpoint does he provide?
2. Celente asserts that we will turn to a simpler life, redistribute our priorities, and broaden our understanding of the term *family*. What does he mean by a simpler life? What will take priority? And how will we define *family* differently?
3. According to Celente, how will humans benefit from the changes he predicts? Had you considered these types of changes before reading the essay? Do you agree with Ce-

lente's point of view? Why or why not? Use the text to illustrate your point.

———————— ✦ ————————

It's January 1, 2000. The world has just celebrated the greatest New Year's Eve party in recorded history. Even cultures that follow different calendars are reveling in the streets. But unlike New Year's parties past, nobody has waited until December 31 to hit the streets. The celebration has been going full blast since Christmas; the world has been psyching itself up for this blowout since 1995, when the symptoms of Millennium Fever were first evident.

For several years religious fanatics and prophets of doom have been preaching the end of the world. And when you look at the events going on around you on New Year's Day, 2000— civil war in Russia, student revolts in the United States, the threat of nuclear terrorism—there's good reason for fear. But Armageddon hasn't happened. The world hasn't gone up in flames.

In fact, there's a strange elation threading through the chaos and disruption. Though the United States and the nest of the world will be going through increasingly troubled times in the immediate future, the first signs of the scientific, artistic, and spiritual renaissance that will shape this new millennium are unmistakable. Those who anticipate and act on the changes taking place will be able to prosper both materially and spiritually. Here are a few trends that will dramatically alter our lives in the coming millennium.

LIVING THE SIMPLE LIFE

Voluntary simplicity, once merely a counterculture ideal, will finally become a reality in the twenty-first century. Simplicity doesn't mean deprivation. Rather, it's old-fashioned Yankee frugality, rediscovered and redesigned for the modern age. Moderation, self-discipline, and spiritual growth will be the personal goals of the future, not material accumulation. As the old saying goes: Use it up, wear it out, make it do, do without.

If you don't really need it, it's a luxury. Not that there's anything wrong with luxuries; it's just that we won't confuse them with necessities.

5   In the 1960s, these ideas and goals seemed quaint and cute. In the new century, however, as cost-cutting corporations continue to lay off vast numbers of workers, many people will have to drastically scale back their lifestyles to survive. Call it *in*voluntary simplicity. But downsizing—currently perceived by the government and the media as a grave problem, and by the downsized as a catastrophe—will prove to be a blessing in disguise in the new millennium. Forced into freedom, millions of us will find ways to take control of our lives and do what we've always wanted to do: change careers, start companies of our own, or become work-at-home freelancers. In 1996, 12 percent of downsized workers started their own businesses, double the rate of 1993.

One major outgrowth of the voluntary simplicity movement will be our desire to grow as much of our own food as possible. But how many people will be able to do this when relatively few Americans live in rural areas where there's room for the type of extensive garden needed to produce a substantial portion of the year's food?

Somewhere around the year 2000, the revelation—and revolution—will come. The lawn! Lawns are everywhere: millions of costly, intensively cared for suburban lawns have been doing nothing but growing grass. But a lawn that's turned into a vegetable patch can produce fresh food.

The trend to convert lawns into gardens will have a significant impact not only on the way we eat but also on how we live and feel. It will be one of the keys to living better for less. Billions of dollars formerly spent on lawn care will either be saved or redeployed into producing fresh food. The American lawn won't disappear entirely, of course. Kids will always romp on them, barbecues will still be held on them. But a significant portion of the nation's arable lawn will be revamped for food production. Just two mature standard fruit trees produce 250 pounds of fruit a year. With millions of downsized or underemployed people struggling to make ends meet, a thousand saved here and a thousand saved there will make a real difference. Even university and corporate campus lawns will be transformed into edible landscapes, providing students and employees with practical, enjoyable, and therapeutic respite from study or work.

MILLENNIUM FAMILY VALUES

Practicing voluntary simplicity, of course, will require a redistribution of our priorities, a rethinking of how we spend our days. Most of us will no longer make the false distinction we used to between "quality" time and the rest of the day. All time will be quality time (except for filling out tax forms and that sort of thing). After all, it takes time to cook a good meal, to play with the kids, to sew a ripped skirt that you once would have thrown away.

With more of us working and spending our free time at home, it's easy to imagine the model twenty-first-century family as Ozzie and Harriet with laptops. But the Nelson family and their real-life counterparts were the products of the 1950s, a time when unparalleled American prosperity allowed the traditional extended family to fragment. In the new millennium, the multigenerational extended family will come together.

Instead of being banished to nursing homes or retirement communities, large numbers of retirees—aging, often ailing, unable to care for themselves or to afford quality care—will move in with their adult children. We'll also see perfectly healthy widowed and divorced parents setting up house alongside their kids—ideally with separate entrances and kitchens to preserve some of the privacy to which we've become accustomed. Family households will sometimes extend to four generations when married or unmarried Generation Xers move back home with their young kids.

Whatever the drawbacks of multigenerational families living together, there will be substantial benefits, too. Healthy grandparents will pull their weight as babysitters. This trend is already strong. In 1994, 44 percent of grandparents spent an average of 650 hours—the equivalent of 81 eight-hour days—taking care of their grandchildren. But more than babysitters, grandparents will also function as home educators. They'll be the modern equivalent of tribal elders who were valued and

10

revered in traditional hunter-gatherer societies for their wisdom and experience.

BACK TO THE BOARDINGHOUSE

The meaning of the word "family" will also broaden beyond that of blood relationships during the twenty-first century. It will come to mean groups of interdependent people—relatives, friends, and neighbors—who share values, goals, responsibilities, and a long-term commitment to one another and their communities. A number of creative (and sometimes desperate) solutions will be found for a wide spectrum of new economic and social challenges.

For example, the 1930s boardinghouse will return in an upgraded version that's designed to meet the needs of modern-day low-income single people. By the year 2010, 31 million people will be living alone. But as disposable incomes continue to fall and the job market tightens, workers of every age will be unable to afford the rents on even studio apartments. While two can live more cheaply than one ten can live substantially cheaper than two, so boardinghouses will reemerge. They'll provide home-cooked communal meals and a congenial family like atmosphere, becoming social oases in an increasingly impersonal world.

15   If the revival of boardinghouses represents an effective defensive tactic against economic changes, "cohousing" will be an offensive long-term strategy. First developed in Denmark in 1976, cohousing combines upscale condominium-style accommodations and privacy with the shared responsibilities and amenities of communes.

The main difference between cohousing and the twentieth century's standard apartment complex or condo is the sharing, which will be tailored to suit the needs of the individuals involved. Most labor-intensive family duties, including meals, child care, elder care, and even education, will be handled communally to some extent. The result will be considerable savings in time and effort, along with pleasant and productive socializing—at least when the personality mix is right. For example, a typical communal dinner arrangement might find residents cooking and serving about once every two weeks, in exchange for having the remaining 13 dinners cooked and served to them.

WHAT YOU HEAR IS WHAT YOU SEE

The videophone, meanwhile, will keep us in touch with faraway relatives. Today when we use the phone, we are still communicating by radio. With the addition of the videophone's visual dimension, long-distance communication will be more like television.

The psychological and social connections fostered by the videophone will transform human interaction. People experience intensely personal, intimate feelings when they can see the person they're talking to; body language comes into play and a person becomes something more than just a disembodied voice. As self-employment, downsizing, and work decentralization keep more and more people in their homes, face-to-face communication will become increasingly uncommon—and therefore increasingly important.

Currently communication industry experts are resisting the videophone idea, pointing to market research that suggests people would rather preserve the comparative anonymity of talking on the telephone. Yet there were similar objections when the telephone answering machine was introduced in the late 1970s. Analysts said that people felt intimidated by the new devices and would not leave messages. In the beginning that was often the case, but today if you call someone and don't get an answering machine to pick up your call, you're probably annoyed. You'll have to call back—an inconvenience. As for the privacy problem, just as a mute button turns off a television's sound a "blind" button will-protect us from Peeping Toms.

MILLENNIUM HEALTH KIT

If you read magazines or watched television in the 1980s and 1990s, it looked as if the whole country was running, pumping iron, and doing aerobics. Sales of running and training shoes

20

soared, and millions bought rowing machines or signed up at gyms. A fitness trend had swept the nation. Or so it seemed. In reality, two-thirds of Americans were overweight as the twentieth century came to a close. If you'd conducted supermarket research, you would have seen battalions of out-of-shape people pushing shopping carts filled with Twinkies, soft drinks, salty snacks, cigarettes, candy, and processed frozen entrees. As for those brisk sales of athletic shoes, 90 percent of the people who bought them did so for comfort and fashion rather than for exercise.

Nevertheless, the health movement, hyped by fitness-gear manufacturers and ballyhooed by the media, is real. And the fitness trend will gather steam as more and more baby boomers begin "previewing": seeing in their parents' aging what lies in store for them.

By the year 2000, getting and staying healthy will no longer be a hobby but a necessity for survival. The health information people need will be available; the difficulty will be distinguishing the gold from the dross. Those who are serious about their millennium resolutions to take better care of themselves will begin by checking into one of the new longevity centers springing up around the country. Longevity centers will be to health what colleges are to education—equal parts spa, health club, hospital, detoxification center, fat farm, and resort. They will be staffed with medical doctors well versed in both state-of-the-art medicine and alternative therapies, as well as nutritionists, acupuncturists, herbalists, chiropractors, and a diverse group of physical, emotional, and spiritual therapists and healers.

Another key player will be the vitamin counselor. While vitamins have been available in supermarkets and health food stores for decades, it was only in the early 1990s that it became apparent that no two people have the same nutritional needs. Effective vitamin counseling must be individualized, just like effective medical advice; a person's age, lifestyle, profession, and eating habits must be taken into account. But most mainstream physicians have had little training in nutrition, and we can't expect knowledgeable advice from minimum-wage clerks at health food stores. Vitamin counselors, on the other hand, will be multidisciplinary practitioners;

they'll have a solid grounding of medical knowledge but won't need four years of medical school. By the year 2000 they will be on their way to becoming as professionalized and as respected as pharmacists.

In an age of intense health awareness, most people will 25 give up their Stair-Masters and stop training for marathons. Hyperactive workouts, while better than nothing, won't be the answer to stress-filled but sedentary lifestyles. Instead, we will integrate our workout routines into our lives. If we haven't given up our lawns altogether, we'll replace our power mowers with high-tech light- weight push mowers.

We'll still use our local gym during the winter and in rainy weather. But instead of doing the usual aerobics, we'll push mowers. And if we're using our lawns to grow food, as most people will be, the physical work of gardening will build bone and muscle.

We'll still use our local gym during the winter and in rainy weather. But instead of doing the usual aerobics, we'll consider becoming "aerobic warriors"—learning an aerobic workout that teaches us self-defense techniques. Since we're putting in the physical effort anyway, why not learn something with a practical application?

COMING ATTRACTIONS

Today, against the dark and violent backdrop of late-twentieth-century life, many of the trends that will soon reshape our lives are not yet apparent. But since writers, musicians, painters, and filmmakers are by nature more sensitive than others to shifts in the tempo of the times, these changes will be quickly reflected in the art of the new century. Just as rock and roll replaced swing and ragtime music, a new genre of millennium music will emerge. It will be upbeat without the anger and despair of today's cutting-edge rock and rap. Painting and sculpture will be revolutionized by the incorporation of virtual reality and computer technology. New, friendly styles of architecture will replace the impersonal cookie-cutter tract housing that has been the norm since the 1950s.

The return of individuality will spell an end to the multi-billion-dollar fashion industry. The bulk of day-to-day apparel will consist of durable mass-produced casual wear. Where appearance matters, the combination of computerization and declining wages will bring custom tailoring back to an affordable price range. The result—personally, designed "smartwear"—will bridge the gap between casual and formal: appearance-enhancing but comfortable.

30   Together, these and numerous other trends will help usher in a new renaissance in thought. It will be an era of intense individuality directed toward common goals. And like the European Renaissance of the fourteenth through seventeenth centuries, the global renaissance ahead will be a time of rich intellectual, philosophical, and artistic achievement—a period of genius in the world's history.

Sample Student Essay

Family Folklore—Has It Really Died Out?

LAURIE SONGHURST

Family folklore, contrary to popular opinion has not died. It is alive and well. Many people tend to get this image in their minds of some longhaired hippy strumming a banjo in the mountains when they hear the term *folklore*. Well, I am here to inform you that this notion of folklore is incorrect. Certainly, that may be one small part of the whole of folklore, but not all that it consists of. Simply put, it is all of the traditions, stories, heirlooms, habits, values, and ways of a family unit or group of people and new ones that family creates and maintains for itself. It permeates every aspect of our lives, whether we are aware of it or not.

Some examples of folklore in our everyday lives are the mannerisms, habits, and values we have learned from our parents. After living with them approximately twenty years, we tend to imitate them in ways we may not even notice. Of course, these ways vary among individuals and their families. Mannerisms and habits of thought or behavior may be negative or positive, and they can include passing on the value of good manners ("please," "thank you," "may I," and "excuse me") or the benefits of thinking of the world as a cup half full instead of half empty. They could also include our exercise and eating habits and the expressions we make, the ways we may stand, and whether or not we talk with our hands.

Other examples of folklore in our lives are the traditions we use during holidays, birthdays, and other special events. These traditions also would vary widely among different families. Included among these traditions would be the foods we eat, serve, and prepare at holidays and special events. For many people, the process of preparing these foods is part of the tradition. For Christmas, people can spend much time planning their preparations. One example is the long-held tradition of cookie baking. Much times goes into deciding what cookies to make year after year. Some make the same ones; some add a new kind every year. The entire process, along with serving and eating the cookies, becomes the tradition.

Turkey at Thanksgiving is another tradition carried out since the Pilgrims came to these shores. Now that is a very long time to honor the same tradition year after year. Some families have ham or something else, but virtually all Americans no doubt honor the tradition of feasting at Thanksgiving. Other people have made traditions out of providing meals for the homeless. This is a wonderful way to express true thanks—by giving out of our abundance.

A tradition that is important to me is the way I celebrate my daughter's birthday. Every year I have an elaborately decorated cake for her. What makes it so special to her is that I get her a cake that is designed to represent something about her personally. When she was younger, it would have a favorite character of hers on it such as Big Bird or Barney. Now that she is older, the cakes represent what she likes to do. This year her cake had a figure skater on it, since my daughter is a figure skater. The cakes are delicious and fun to eat, but, more important, they serve to identify my daughter as a member of my family and as an individual; they let her know we recognize who she truly is.

All of the things mentioned earlier are examples of folklore in our everyday lives. There are also reasons we engage in these different rituals and traditions. One reason folklore is used is to help shape us as individuals. When we begin our own, new traditions, we separate ourselves from our family to forge a new one. We often take the opportunity when we set out to live alone for the first time, get married, or have a new baby to create new ways of doing things that reinforce our sense of family and help us establish who we have become.

On the other hand, traditions give us a sense of community, of belonging to a group. We were created to need relationships for fulfillment, and our traditions can strengthen the bonds of a group. Traditions can also fulfill our need for stability in this unstable world. Every time we repeat them, they become more familiar, and this familiarity gives us the feeling of stability and security.

I know from experience that folklore is still being carried out today. It is not outdated. Now that I have a better understanding of what it really entails, I am having fun focusing on my family's folklore. I have even begun the process of restoring wayward family members to old traditions and making an effort to create more of my own traditions. There is a history to our folklore; it solidifies our identities and strengthens family bonds. It helps us "live on," and so, too, shall it.

My Thoughts in Writing

1. Songhurst asserts that family folklore is alive and well. What evidence does she provide that this is the case? Which piece of evidence is the most convincing? Why?
2. Songhurst tells us that the tradition of celebrating her daughter's birthday serves a number of purposes. What does this tradition entail? What purposes does it serve?
3. In conclusion, Songhurst mentions two ways she is keeping folklore alive in her own family. How is she helping folklore retain its vitality? How do our own lives relate to the life of folklore? Why do you think Songhurst concludes with this point?

The Readings Come Together

1. In her essay, Songhurst asserts that traditions offer "stability in an unstable world." How does this statement and the evidence she provides for it relate to Celente's essay and his point that we will return to more traditional values and ways of living despite the chaos of the new millennium?
2. Both Kandell and Knight feel a need to return to places that hold cultural and family memories or where family members live. How are their experiences in these places similar? How are they different? How are the writers similarly affected by their returns to these places?
3. The essays in this chapter focus on the value of tradition in cultural communities today. Compare and contrast how the authors feel about the value of tradition and the state of the particular types of folklore they discuss. How do their works come together to emphasize the value of cultural roots?
4. In their essays both Bragg and Kandell discuss the loss of tradition. How do their works illustrate the effects of that loss on others? Do they offer hope for their traditions? Explain your answers.
5. In Knight's work, there is a longing for familial connections. How does this longing relate to the longing in Giovanni's poem? How do the granddaughter's actions in Giovanni's poem relate to the speaker's action and emotions in Knight's poem? How do the poems come together to form a common message about the value of family and tradition?
6. Both Susteren and Gladstone write of traditions that are still alive and well within their particular cultural communities. How have these traditions

managed to stay vital? What has each community done to maintain its tradition? What purpose does each tradition serve?

There's Something More out There

Part I

At-Home Activity

This activity requires interviewing. Review your journal and make a list of all the people you have interviewed regarding the folklore in their lives. Then, create a list of interview questions pertaining to the subject of this chapter, the future of folklore. When you are satisfied with the interview questions you have created, use them to interview each individual on your list. If you have a tape recorder, record each interview and then transcribe the interviews into your journal. If you do not have a tape recorder, simply write the interviewees' answers down in your journal. Try to be as accurate in wording the answers given as possible. Use complete sentences.

Part II

Classroom Storytelling Session

Study Experiences   Sharing Family and Community Folklore Encounters/ Imagining a Folklore Future or a Folklore-less Life. With your classmates, discuss the way folklore influences your lives. Determine the role of folklore in the future? How would your lives be affected if folklore ceased to exist?

Part III

Journal Entry

Option 1   Imagine that a family or community member wishes to discontinue or no longer be a part of a long-standing tradition. In your journal, write a letter to that person arguing the necessity of keeping the tradition alive or the importance of his or her continuing participation in it. Use both reason and logic and appeals to emotion in your attempts to convince that person of the tradition's significance to your family or community or the person's importance to the tradition as an individual.

Option 2   Choose one tradition your family or community has discarded over the years and write a letter to your family or community members in which you try to persuade them to reactivate this tradition. In your attempts to persuade them, you might mention the traditions that have withstood the years and remind them of such traditions' importance and the purpose(s) they serve. How is the lost tradition similar to the ones in which they still engage? How is it different? Why did it disappear? How might your family or community return to this tradition? Would it have to be changed? Why or why not?

Part IV

Writing Assignments

Using one or more of the reading selections to approach your topic.

Option 1   Imagine you are a small-town newspaper columnist. Write an editorial illustrating your belief that, contrary to popular opinion, family/community folklore is—as it was in the past—alive and well and a valuable contributor to group and individual identity and one's sense of self and/or community. Or take another angle and write a brief editorial illustrating your belief that family/community folklore is dying out. Using MLA documentation format to identify and properly credit the sources of your proof of your assertions. Your thesis should make clear whether you think this is a good or bad thing, and your conclusion should either make suggestions or predictions for the future based on your essay's central assertion.

Option 2   Write an essay in which you argue that those members (or member) of your family/community who regularly engage in creative self-expressive traditions should be viewed as role models for members of the younger generation. In your essay, identify how the tradition serves the individual and, by extension, the family/community as a whole.

Option 3   Using any of the selections from this chapter (or a source approved by your instructor) as your principal outside source, write an essay in which you argue that progress (or change, such as technological advances) should not mean the loss of a folklore-engaged world. In your essay, provide examples of those individuals who use folk traditions to round out their lives. Identify how the traditions serve these individuals and, by extension, the family/community as a whole.

Brunvand, Jan Harold. 1986. *The Study of American Folklore: An Introduction*. 3d ed. New York: Norton.

Zeitlin, Steve J., Amy J. Kotkin, and Holly Cutting Baker, eds. 1982. *A Celebration of American Family Folklore: Tales and Traditions from the Smithsonian Collection*. New York: Pantheon.

Bragg, Rick, "The Blues Is Dying in the Place It Was Born" from *The New York Times*, April 22, 2001. Reprinted by permission of The New York Times.

Brodeur, Nicole, "Meaning of hunt lost from afar." By Nicole Brodeur, *Seattle Times* staff columnist. May 20, 1999. Copyright © 1999 Seattle Times Company. Used with permission.

Celente, Gerald, "Welcome to the Millennium" from *Trends 2000* by Gerald Celente. Copyright © 1997 by Gerald Celente. By permission of Warner Books, Inc.

Giovanni, Nikki, "Legacies" from *My House* by Nikki Giovanni. Copyright © 1972 by Nikki Giovanni. Reprinted by permission of HarperCollins Publisher Inc.

Giovanni, Nikki, "On Holidays and How to Make Them Work" from *Sacred Cows and other Edibles* by Nikki Giovanni. Copyright © 1988 by Nikki Giovanni. Reprinted by permission of HarperCollins Publishers Inc.

Gladstone, Valerie, "Dance: Enriching Lives by Relearning African Culture" from *The New York Times*, May 20, 2001. Reprinted by permission of The New York Times.

Glaser, Michael S., "Preparations for Seder." First appeared in *A Lover's Eye* by Michael S. Glaser, The Bunny and the Crocodile Press © 1989 Michael S. Glaser. Reprinted here with permission from the author.

Hampl, Patricia, "Grandmother's Sunday Dinner" from *A Romantic Education* by Patricia Hampl. Copyright © 1981